D1568785

Most Catholics know that Protestant "private interpretation" of Scripture leads to grave errors. But how many know exactly what those errors are — or what the Church really *does* teach about the Bible?

This smoothly written treatment of Catholic "Bible basics" by a renowned Scripture scholar shows Catholics how — and how not — to read and interpret the Word of God, which, after all, He entrusted to His Church. It also shows how to refute the errors of both Protestants and secular Bible critics.

Cuthbert Lattey, the respected Jesuit whose scholarly research was crucial to the Westminster Version of the Bible, was widely praised for this popular 1944 guidebook:

"One of the most valuable and effective popular handbooks on the introduction to Sacred Scripture."
— *American Ecclesiastical Record*

"The fruit of years of scholarly devotion to the Scriptures."
—*Theological Studies*

"Deserves high praise as a useful summary of, and valuable commentary on, biblical questions of major importance, presented in a very readable manner."
— *Irish Ecclesiastical Record*

BACK TO THE BIBLE
SOME VITAL ISSUES

By
C. LATTEY, S.J.

With a Foreword by
THE MOST REVEREND
RICHARD DOWNEY, D.D., Ph.D., LL.D.
ARCHBISHOP OF LIVERPOOL

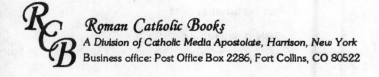

Roman Catholic Books
A Division of Catholic Media Apostolate, Harrison, New York
Business office: Post Office Box 2286, Fort Collins, CO 80522

DE LICENTIA SUPERIORUM ORDINIS

NIHIL OBSTAT:
ERNESTUS C. MESSENGER, Ph.D.
Censor Deputatus.

IMPRIMATUR:
E. MORROGH BERNARD, Vic. Gen.

WESTMONASTERII,
die 12a Augusti, 1944.

First published in 1944

ISBN 0-912141-41-7

CONTENTS

Thou sayest, ' I am rich, and have grown wealthy and have need of nothing,' and knowest not that thou art the wretched and pitiable and poor and blind and naked one. Therefore I counsel thee to buy of me refined gold out of the fire, that thou mayest be made rich ; and white garments, that thou mayest be clothed withal, and that the shame of thy nakedness be not made manifest ; and eye-salve to anoint thine eyes, that thou mayest see. Whomso I love, I rebuke and chastise ; be earnest therefore, and repent.

Behold, I stand at the door and knock. If any one hear my voice and open the door, I will come in to him, and I will sup with him, and he with me.

As for him that conquereth, I will give him to sit with me upon my throne, as I myself conquered, and sat down with my Father on His throne.

(Apoc. iii, 17–21.)

FOREWORD

BY

THE MOST REVEREND RICHARD DOWNEY, D.D., Ph.D., LL.D., ARCHBISHOP OF LIVERPOOL

FR. CUTHBERT LATTEY, S.J., needs no introduction to biblical scholars; he is well known far beyond the confines of this country as a past master in hermeneutics and exegesis, and for his valuable research work in connection with the editing of the Westminster Version of the Scriptures. The present book is not intended exclusively for Catholics, but is designed to promote a general return to the Bible, chiefly by explaining the fundamental principles at stake and the outstanding difficulties in their application. It is intended for any reasonably intelligent reader, but should give even scholars matter for thought.

One sound principle of interpretation is worth a hundred particular applications; like divine Providence it ' reaches mightily from end to end and disposes all things sweetly.' For this reason it is probable that Part One of the present work is the most important section in an important book; its worth is to be judged not by the length of the treatment (though this is not inconsiderable), but by the depth of its content. It deals with the principles of sober exegesis, indispensable principles which cut out error at the root. And indeed the exposition of the nature of biblical truth is vital if the Sacred Scriptures are to be restored to the repute they once enjoyed outside the Church, and if the principles of intelligent interpretation are to be preserved and propagated within. The Catholic exegete is not prepared, nor ever will be prepared, to subscribe to the formula of his

FOREWORD

non-Catholic fellows : ' The tradition of the inerrancy of the
Bible . . . cannot be maintained in the light of the knowledge
now at our disposal ; '[1] his standpoint is described in un-
compromising terms by Pope Leo XIII : " Inspiration not
only is essentially incompatible with error, but excludes and
rejects it as absolutely and necessarily as it is impossible that
God Himself, the supreme Truth, can utter that which is
not true."[2] Yet we might ask, though without the despairing
scepticism of Pilate, ' What is truth ? ' Truth is one but
its presentation is various—in poem, for instance, in allegory,
in historical narrative. The defence of biblical truth,
therefore, leads us perforce to a consideration and intelligent
appreciation of literary *genre* which alone can bring us to
the goal of all interpretation—the meaning which the author
intended to convey. If this procedure be suspect (though
only by abuse has it brought suspicion upon itself) let the
words of the present Holy Father himself be its advocate :

' The principal rule in interpretation, as St. Augustine says, is
to establish what the author was intending to say ; and if this be
borne in mind, serious error is ruled out. It is often not so
obvious from the words of ancient orientals as from those of men
of our own time exactly what the literal sense of a statement may
be. The intended meaning of these ancient authors is not therefore to be determined only by the rules of grammar or philology,
nor is it always clear from the context. The interpreter must also
consider the mentality of those remote centuries and, with the aid
of history, archæology, ethnology and other sciences, must clearly
discern the nature of the literary forms natural to men of those days.
What these forms were can only be determined after an accurate
study of ancient oriental literature. Investigation carried out in
the last few decades has thrown clearer light on the nature of
these forms, whether they be those used in poetical composition,
in prescribing laws, or in writing history. . . . The knowledge
and exact appraisement of ancient modes of speech and writing
will indeed dispose of many allegations made against the truth and
historical value of the Bible.[3] '

[1] *Doctrine in the Church of England.* London. S.P.C.K., 1922.
[2] Encyclical *Providentissimus Deus*, 1893.
[3] Encyclical *Divino Afflante Spiritu*, 1943.

FOREWORD

In this field there is much yet to accomplish, and it will be accomplished usefully and securely only if right principles are duly preserved.

Part Two needs no apology for the relatively full treatment which it accords to the 'Documentary Hypothesis.' In truth, this is no exclusively specialist question, nor do its natural and actual developments limit themselves to the Mosaic books; quite the contrary. The theory of late and multiple documents is now axiomatic among the great majority of non-Catholic scholars. Guaranteed in substance by names like Sellin and König and (in this country) S. R. Driver, Briggs and others, the theory refuses to be ignored; the lexicographers, too, boldly characterize their vocabulary: ' document J,' or 'E,' 'D,' 'P.' The interested and intelligent non-Catholic layman, capable of assessing only a fraction of the argument, has no choice but to follow. Five or ten years later, popular articles duly present the conclusions (without the premisses) to a larger public, and so by bold assertion, or by covert assumption, the public mind is formed and the public credit of the Bible disparaged and defamed. Moreover, the Documentary Theory does not stop at the Pentateuch, its disruptive offshoots creep over and into the whole biblical structure—the Law, the Psalms, the Prophets. The divine revelation measured out to the Hebrew people is represented as nothing more than the growing spiritual consciousness of a religiously perceptive race; monotheism becomes the purely natural development of henotheism by which Yahweh from being the national deity passes to supremacy among the gods and finally to unique Godhead. What should be the answer of the Catholic? ' Credo!' of course, but surely he owes it to the Church, to his non-Catholic neighbour, to himself, that his belief should be a *fides quaerens intellectum*? It is with this high purpose that the learned author fronts the problem. He does so in favourable season; the phalanx is wavering that stretches from d'Astruc to our present day for, as Sellin admits, we are in ' a period of transition and uncertainty.' The author's approach goes, as it must, by hard ways, but it leads to the weakest points of a complicated defence-system once confidently believed unassailable. His whole exposition fully justifies the caution with which sound Catholic criticism has always received the dogmatisms of the Wellhausen tradition.

A discussion of New Testament problems follows in Part Three where attention is drawn to the historical character of the Gospel story and to the reliability of its four presentations. The mutual relationship of the first three Gospels has long been and will continue to be a battleground of opinions. Had this been a purely literary question it would have found no place in a short work which is intended to deal only with problems that are pressing and practical ; but it is not a purely literary question. Here, too, as in the case of the Old Testament documentary hypothesis, the leaven of Hegelian evolution has been working in the schools of liberal criticism. Thus, Mark, the simplest form of the Gospel story, unpolished in style, untheological in content, has become the more complex organism which received the name of " The Gospel according to St. Matthew.' By a process ironically similar this theory itself has now evolved from a working hypothesis into a postulate. It is not, we have said, merely a literary question or a matter of historical curiosity only. In the home of its adoption it is big with the possibilities of the gravest consequence. What, for instance, is to become of the Petrine text of Matt. xvi, 17–19, absent from Mark's Gospel ? It has long ago been vindicated by textual criticism, is it to fall a victim to the higher criticism ? Is it an addition forced upon the Marcan account by the evolving self-consciousness of the later Christian community ? This book does not refuse the challenge. It is not unnatural that a complex problem should call for a complex solution and the ' Synoptic Question ' is no exception, but the case is presented clearly and in a way which satisfies both the demands of historical tradition and the data furnished by the Gospels themselves.

Next we have the Gospel of St. John, the stamping-ground of liberalism rampant : John was a disciple of the Apostle, John never saw the Apostle ; John was a Judeo-

FOREWORD

Christian, John was an ethnico-Christian; John was a Gnostic and an adversary of Gnosticism; John was one and many :—liberalism may well look with despair on the ruins it has made. A robust vindication of the authenticity and of the historical character of the fourth Gospel is the only remedy, and it presents insoluble difficulty only to those whom free thought constrains to reject the supernatural and to deny the divinity of Christ.

There remains the admirable presentation of St. Paul, who is described as ' a great man upon any standard, in himself and in the effect produced upon the world by his life-work.' Fr. Lattey brings out very clearly St. Paul's great synthesis of unity : our unity with Christ, and in Him with the Father and with each other, and this unity with Christ both individual and corporate, through the Church. The thesis is opportune, as St. Paul is nowadays so frequently invoked by non-Catholics as the protagonist of disunity, when he was in reality the apostle of unity *par excellence*. Fr. Lattey's brief but lucid treatment of this vital theme is in itself a valuable contribution to the interpretation of the Pauline epistles.

This book deserves to be widely read, and will help to restore the Bible to the proud place which it formerly held in the religious life of the nation. Of late years it has fallen into neglect for a variety of reasons, one being the ignorant notion that ' Science ' has in some mysterious way discredited it. Fr. Lattey's volume is indeed a timely contribution to the Present Problems series.

PART I

GENERAL

I

INTRODUCTORY

THIS work is published as one of the ' Present Problems '
series ; and the question may be asked ; ' how can the Bible
be reckoned a present-day problem ? ' Some perhaps will
just say that it has been exploded, and there is an end of the
matter. And yet—is there an end ? Will there ever be an
end ? Whatever a few reckless spirits may think, the better
and saner part of mankind will ever be haunted by those
sacred words, and even in depths of misery and guilt, men
will hear a voice they thought to have forgotten, calling to
something better, and awaking once more a nobler self.

Others there may be, to whom for an opposite reason the
whole matter may seem far too simple to be called a problem.
These are they who still have full faith in the Bible, and reap
much spiritual help from it, and are content to leave it to the
learned to dispute over any difficulties that may be found
in it, without being troubled thereat themselves. In itself
this is an admirable frame of mind, but may perhaps take too
little heed of the Apostle's words, found in the Bible itself :
' The charity of Christ constraineth us ' (2 Cor. v, 14). And
indeed, many other sayings of Christ and His apostles can be
found to urge us to take thought for the world outside, however satisfied we may feel with our own position ; the closer
we are to Christ, the more ready we must be to love those

around us, even to the death. Only a little before writing these lines, I had read in the *Times* of April 24, 1943, the Archbishop of Canterbury's words in his Good Friday broadcast : ' The decline in honesty has been very sharp and steep. Our standard of conduct in matters of sex is very lax.' And in the *Church Times* of May 14, 1943, Lord Davidson is reported to have dwelt ' on the degree to which the war had revealed England to be virtualy pagan ' (p. 251). Both these are courageous utterances, and must surely be viewed by all earnest Christians as summing up a terrible problem. The last war does not seem, upon the whole, to have had any marked influence for good, for any impulse in that direction seems to have been outweighed by a reaction into a scoffing boredom. The present war has let loose powers of evil which it will be difficult to control, even with the help of the spiritual revival which in various quarters has certainly made itself apparent.

Where then does the Bible come in ? To a large number in Great Britain religion means the Bible. It is true that it is far less known, and even far less respected, than at the end of the last century. The millions upon millions that have been spent upon so-called education have largely been spent in defiance of God, in defiance of the family, and even to a large extent in defiance of reason, in the sense that too little attention has been devoted to the training of the intellect, so that our modern citizen is all too easily led by the cinema and the demagogue and the cheap press, and is all too happy to have his thinking done for him. And yet, many a one would not willingly forfeit his claim to the title of Christian, and some respect is left for what his forefathers Protestant and Catholic, venerated as the word of God.

And there lies the main problem : it is no small one. May it not be possible, through the Bible, to lead back to religion and the worship of God many whose faith has become dim and their hope faint and their charity cold ? May they not be brought to ponder more seriously all that Jesus Christ is in Himself, and all that He should mean for them ? His words have a spiritual savour all their own, and, with the help of God's grace, woo powerfully the heart and head of all who will pay reverent heed to them.

I am writing this book as a Catholic, with full belief in the Catholic Church; but it is my hope that it may be of spiritual help even outside the Catholic fold. What a change of front we have seen! At first the Church was accused of making too little of the Bible, but now she is largely accused of taking it too seriously. So too it has been in some other matters; she is now accused of insisting inhumanly upon the doctrine of eternal punishment, whereas the early Protestants went much farther, setting forth a God who pushed ruthlessly His helpless victims into Hell, rejecting fiercely even the consoling doctrine of Purgatory. But the Church does take the Scriptures seriously, every word of them, and will not give up what she knows herself to find in them; she recognizes her right and duty to guard and defend them, and no modern criticism will make her budge, where she is satisfied that she has the mind of her Divine Author.

It is impossible to be a good Catholic without wishing that the rest of men may become good Catholics too. It would indeed be a dreadful frame of mind, to believe that one has the key of knowledge, and not to desire to open the door wide to all men: to know that one possesses the truth, and to be so wanting in love towards one's fellow-men as not to wish to share it. Gladly, therefore, I confess, not only my own faith, but my longing to share it with all men. None the less, it is not the object of this book to effect conversions, but rather to strengthen whatever belief in the Scriptures the reader may already possess. The more divine truth there is in him the better, even though much be lacking. I am not even writing primarily for Catholics, though I hope that what is written may prove of service to them also. Had I been writing primarily for Catholics, I should have come more directly to the matter in hand, without insisting so strongly upon various preliminary considerations and presuppositions.

The selection and arrangement and treatment of the matter in the book has therefore been governed by its primary aim. I have tried to keep in mind throughout the point of view of the non-Catholic, and such difficulties as are likely to appeal to him. It has of course been out of the question to touch upon all the biblical problems that can arise ; but I hope that it will be recognized that I have touched upon most that are of major importance. I have not been anxious to urge my own views, partly because considerations of space would often forbid my doing full justice to them ; my object has rather been to show that it is not necessary to reject the Bible as unworthy of God, whether by reason of false statements or of encouragement to vice. It is not possible to bring out in full relief all the divine beauty and spiritual influence of Holy Writ : in that respect no treatise can ever do it justice : but at least the difficulties which hide its heavenly charm may be sufficiently removed, with God's grace, to let us believe that perfect vision would behold perfect beauty.

I have said that I am not writing primarily for Catholics ; nevertheless I should certainly wish to include them among my readers. Sometimes they seem to feel almost an instinctive dread of Holy Scripture, the result no doubt of centuries of controversy ; they have been happy and content within the Church, and have no desire to begin wrangling about texts and such things, especially now, when they are so liable to be confronted with blank contradictions of Scripture rather than with rival interpretations. They may even have a feeling that devotion to the Scriptures is something rather Protestant, or perhaps confess to some little fear that too much attention to the Old Testament may end in some temptation to their faith.

Against such an attitude, as one who has loved the Scriptures from his youth : as one who has never received anything but encouragement to love and study them from his own religious order and from the Church : as one who has felt no difficulty, due to Holy Scripture, in his faith or spiritual life, but only immense help and lively encouragement, I feel bound to protest. Even of the Old Testament the Apostle writes that ' whatsoever things were written aforetime were written for our instruction, that through patience and through the comfort of the Scriptures we may have hope ' (Rom. xv, 4).

BACK TO THE BIBLE

And at the end of his Encyclical *Spiritus Paraclitus* Pope Benedict XV declares that ' we desire for all the children of the Church that, penetrated and strengthened by the sweetness of the Sacred Scriptures, they may attain to the surpassing knowledge of Jesus Christ.' In the gospels we have Christ Himself speaking and acting, and St. Paul in his epistles tells us all that Christ should be for us ; the prophets foreshadow Him, besides teaching much else of profound value. The Bible should be read intelligently and in proper order, after some little preparation ; where help is earnestly sought from it, help will be found.

It is to be hoped that this book itself may promote a right appreciation of Holy Writ, though any book that serves the purpose should be welcome. It should also prove a help to Catholics to have those foundations of faith in the Scriptures strengthened, which no Christian ought to lack. In these difficult days more instruction in religion is needed by all ; and the importance of the matter will suggest an apostolic motive for greater attention to Holy Writ on the part of Catholics, since they ought to be the light of the world, not only by their good works, but also by virtue of their knowledge of the truth. It is indeed consoling to find that Catholics in actual fact are taking an increasing interest in the Scriptures, and are showing a greater devotion towards them, at a time when so many are showing ever less concern for the sacred writings ; it is much to be hoped that the biblical movement will long continue to make good progress, as indeed it bids fair to do.

II

REASON

WHEN reflecting upon the biblical difficulties of our time, I am always brought back to the same conviction, that the greatest and fundamental difficulties do not arise from history or archæology, or from any part of what may be called strictly biblical studies, but from the presuppositions which have established themselves in the minds of a large number of biblical scholars. They may flatter themselves that they are impartial, that they are merely doing their best to discover to which side the balance of historical evidence inclines ; but after much reading and listening I am left in many cases with the ineluctable conclusion that they are deluding themselves.

The acid test is to be found in the evidence for miracles. This evidence is stronger in some cases than in others ; and again, it may likewise be called inherently more probable. A supposed miracle may make an instant appeal to us ; even the unbeliever may feel that, if there are to be miracles at all, this is the kind of miracle that he would welcome and approve. St. Luke, the tender-hearted evangelist who brings out so well Christ's compassion for the sorrows of men, alone narrates the raising from the dead of the only son of the widow of Nain (Luke vii), and none can fail to perceive the heavenly beauty of the story. On the other hand, the very nature of the miracle may add something to the difficulty which some feel about the swallowing of Jonah by the whale ; or again, in the transportation of Habakkuk to Daniel in the lions' den in Dan. xiv (' Bel and the Dragon ').

To such as do not find in their faith a special motive for the acceptance of such miracles (so far as the Faith obliges

B

any thereto) the story of them may seem incredible upon its own merits, almost apart from any appeal to evidence. But this is not the attitude to which I am here taking exception ; for in itself it is compatible with the acceptance of miracles in general as a real possibility, and of individual miracles in particular. But if no miracle whatever is ever accepted in any circumstances, if no narrative of miracle is ever accepted as fact until the miraculous element in it has been explained away, if modern ' progress ' is thought to comprise the eliminating of any miraculous element from human history, then the person who adopts this standpoint and imagines that he is weighing the evidence impartially is deluding himself. And the same verdict may be passed on one who absolutely excludes the possibility of a divine revelation : who has made up his mind that whatever else God may do, He certainly must not be allowed to deal with His creature in such a way as to communicate to him truths of which he would not otherwise be aware.

And thus we are brought face to face with the question of God. It is the supreme question nowadays, not merely for intellectual but also for practical reasons. Even the question of the Divinity of Christ takes the second place when compared with the question whether there be a God at all. And by ' God ' is not here meant a God in nothing but name, but what may be shortly expressed as a ' personal ' God : a supreme Being distinct from all other beings, with intellect and will, or rather, who *is* His own intellect and will. If such a Being be once believed to exist, revelation and miracle can present no serious difficulty to a thinking man ; it is fitting rather than otherwise that He should take an interest in His own creatures. It is only too evident that the idea of God, even as known by the natural light of reason, has become much obscured in the world at large, with the inevitable result that His effective intervention in the world has come to be looked upon as something almost incredible.

On the other hand, in the Vatican Council, Pope Pius IX, ' with the bishops of the whole world sitting and judging with us,' decreed along with them :

REASON

'The Holy Catholic Apostolic Roman Church believes and confesses that there is one true and living God, Creator and Lord of heaven and earth, almighty, everlasting, immense, incomprehensible, infinite in intellect and will and all perfection. Inasmuch as He is one single, altogether simple and unchangeable spiritual substance, He is to be proclaimed in fact and essence distinct from the world, in Himself and of Himself most happy, and unspeakably exalted above all things which exist or can be conceived beside Him.'[1]

This is not the place wherein to comment at length upon the above decree; it may be enough to refer the reader to *Principles of Natural Theology* in the Stonyhurst Philosophical Series, by my late colleague Father G. H. Joyce, S.J.[2] Nor is it possible to treat of some other philosophical truths of fundamental importance, such as the human soul and the nature of knowledge. It is idle to propound a religion that has not a sound philosophy to support it. Philosophy itself cannot take the place of religion or theology, but in the long run it tends to subvert any system that has not come to terms with it. Protestantism in particular has been to some extent indifferent or even hostile to philosophy, and has found in this a source of weakness; those who hold Protestantism true should have worked out its implications in philosophy, if they did not wish its hold upon assent to remain precarious.

It is, indeed, probably to be counted a loss to religion, that there seems to be little coherent philosophy taught at our universities. By 'coherent' I here mean one that considers the main issues of human life, so far as they can be resolved by unaided reason. If I may speak of Oxford, seeing that I know it best, the study of Plato and Aristotle seems to have been originally introduced into the 'Greats' course in order to complete the picture of classic culture presented by the poets, orators and historians. But under the shadow of Plato and Aristotle have crept in a queer crew of German idealists, who certainly have less claim to be there than such

[1] Denzinger, *Enchiridion Symbolorum*, Sess. III, ch. 1, ed. 14–15. Herder, 1922: no. 1782.
[2] Longmans, ed. 3, 1934.

BACK TO THE BIBLE

a one as St. Thomas Aquinas, who may be said to stand in the direct line of descent. In any case we have here (speaking roughly) only Logic and Ethics ; Psychology is a forlorn Cinderella, and little attempt has been made to work out any coherent scheme of time and space and matter and life, such as would deserve the title of Cosmology. Natural Theology, the study of what reason has to tell us about God, appears to be the most neglected of all, though it is the most relevant for this book. It would be a far-reaching reform if degrees in philosophy were reserved for a systematic study of it, embracing the subjects mentioned above.

It might in this way become a unifying influence, with the aim to combine into a synthesis not merely the *disiecta membra* of philosophy itself, but also university studies as a whole, which have been much rent apart by premature specialization. The doctor is apt to look upon man as no more than a piece of animated mutton : the lawyer is prone to look upon his laws as closing any discussion of human conduct, without leaving room for any claims of morality : for such misguided thinkers one is tempted to suggest the motto, ' We have a law, and according to the law he must die ' (John xix, 7). The historian also may have his taboos, not to be violated by any divine intervention, even if sometimes we have to tell him that he is wiping out history itself.

It must, I think, be reckoned righteousness to the school-men of all ages, that they have always striven to make a synthesis of knowledge, even if at times they have been over-hasty in their methods. It is in keeping with this that they have been quick to see the logical implications of views put before them. The failure to do so is to some extent characteristic of our time, and is liable to lead to great confusion of thought. The matter is so important that it is worth while to adduce a couple of instances, and in both cases from writers of whose learned scholarship and religious earnestness there could be no doubt. In 1927 the late Dr. Streeter published a work entitled *Reality, a new correlation of science and religion* (Macmillan), in which he early abandoned the principle of causality, writing as follows :

' This taking for granted that for every event there *must* be some cause, Kant explains by saying that the peculiar quality of the relation we call causation is one which is read into experience by the experiencing mind. To this particular contention of Kant there has never, so far as I know, been given any satisfactory answer ' (pp. 20–1).

After which we had better come at once to his idea of God :

' The Universe is a coherent system—otherwise Science could not interpret It in terms of Law—and It is the expression of a Living Power ; then is It not of living organisms the most highly organized of all ? Unless, then, we are to conceive that Life as less vital than our own, we must ascribe to it that element in personality which makes it a focus of synthetic activity, originative, directive, co-ordinative. We must not think of It as an " ocean of life," or even as a " stream of consciousness," but as a closely knit, highly centralized, self-consistent, fully self-conscious, eternally creative Unity. That is, we must not regard the Ultimate Reality as merely in a vague way personal ; we must ascribe to *IT*, what, for want of a richer word, we can only call Individuality ' (p. 137 : capitals as in originals).

In the first place one might ask, how can this *IT* be supposed active, originative, directive, closely knit or eternally creative, without supposing causation to be at work ? But an even graver question is how this ' Universe ' can be personal and fully self-conscious, and possess individuality, when the human beings in it are so well aware of a self-consciousness and individuality all their own, and other than those of their fellows ? We might even wonder—but with all seriousness and respect—how Dr. Streeter came to write a book on ' Restatement and Reunion,' if unity be already possessed to such an incredible degree.

Another striking example of the failure to correlate the thoughts of a single mind is to be found in *The Ideas of the Fall and of Original Sin*, by the late Dr. N. P. Williams (Longmans, 1927), who likewise died prematurely to the loss of Oxford. The sub-title runs, ' A Historical and Critical Study,' and is justified by much valuable matter of that kind ; but the lectures conclude with the startling hypothesis of a ' pre-cosmic vitiation of the whole Life-Force, at the very beginning of cosmic evolution.'

' To avoid both dualism and an infinite regress, we must suppose that the Life-Force corrupted itself—which means that we must conceive it as having been, at its creation, personal and free—a self-conscious *anima mundi*, like the " only-begotten universe-god " of Plato's *Timæus*. The Father of all things must have created this World-Soul good ; but at the beginning of time, in some transcendental and incomprehensible manner, it turned away from Him and towards Self, thus staining its own essence and, perhaps, forfeiting self-consciousness, which it has only regained after æons of myopic striving, in sporadic fragments, which are the separate minds of men ' (pp. xxxiv–xxxv).

It has seemed clearer and shorter to take this extract from the admirable ' Synopsis of Contents,' rather than from the text itself. It will readily be seen what grave psychological— not to say theological—problems this hypothesis raises. The Life-Force itself appears to bear some relation to Dr. Streeter's *IT*, but how such a presumably immaterial soul can have broken up into fragments, how the perfection of the fellowship of all beings will finally express itself ' in the redintegrated consciousness of the general Soul ' (p. 530), must be left for those to explain who can see no essential distinction between matter and mind.

It is this failure to develop anything like a co-ordinated system of thought that vitiates a large part of our national education, in which a reckless specialization entrusts the teaching of individual subjects to those who have no concep- tion of truth as a whole. This intellectual flaw in the teaching necessarily involves a moral flaw, in the sense that no sufficient motive can be offered for good conduct. The tone of a school, and still more of a particular schoolroom, can be godless, even when prayers are being regularly said to God ; and the in- tellectual and moral growth of the child cannot but be stunted, where there is no serious attempt to make the religious develop- ment keep pace with them. Far other was the mind of Him who said, ' Suffer the little children to come unto me, hinder them not ; for of such is the kingdom of God ' (Mark x, 14).

III

REVELATION

HOLY Scripture distinguishes three main stages in the history of true religion : the period before Moses, the period from Moses to Christ, the period from Christ till the end of the time. In none of these periods was man left to merely 'natural' religion. Even a purely anthropological study of primitive religion, without any appeal to theological considerations, appears to point to revelation as its starting-point.[1] It seems very unlikely, though not demonstrably false, that Adam and Eve should be understood to have been left for a while to merely natural religion ; in any case they are represented as falling from a highly privileged position of intercourse with God and freedom from lust. The biblical theology of the Fall is to be found mainly in Rom. v, 12–21. Even the period between the Fall and the promulgation of the Mosaic Law was a time in which the patriarchs and others are said to have received divine favours and guidance. The Mosaic Law itself involved elaborate ritual and constant revelation, although upon the dogmatic side it was far simpler than the Christian faith. Finally He who in various ways had made many partial manifestations of divine truth through the prophets spoke to mankind through His Son, a favour beyond anything that could have been hoped or imagined.

God's purpose, we may thus say, has never been merely natural religion ; and it is a wrong method of approach to look for merely natural religion in what He has instituted.

[1] *Cf.* W. Schmidt, *Origin and Growth of Religion,* Engl. transl. Methuen, 1931.

BACK TO THE BIBLE

Once we have realized that religion as we find it in the Bible has been of divine and not of human institution, we must be content to study what God *did* do, without pretending that He was *bound* to do it. We must not try to tie Him down to our own petty conceits. Even more important nowadays, however, is the question what He *could* do. Stress has already been laid upon this. Strictly speaking, some knowledge of God should precede the study of the Bible, which however has much to tell of God, even as known by unaided reason, if only the reader will not harden his mind and heart against it.

What we actually find is that before the Mosaic Law the patriarchs were their own priests and themselves offered sacrifice ; moreover Melchizedek (Gen. xiv, 18) and Jethro (Exod. xviii, 1, 12) were recognized as priests of the true God even before the institution of the levitical priesthood. The religion of the Old Testament will perhaps be understood best from a summary contrast with the Catholic religion to-day. Although provision was made for the reception of gentile proselytes, it was essentially a national religion, whereas the Catholic religion claims by its very name to be universal. The Chosen People constituted a theocracy, subject in all things to Jehovah's revealed will, for the execution of which the secular ruler himself was in great part responsible : thus, Moses himself, though a Levite, was not a priest, and several kings, especially David, are commended for the care which they exercised over the national worship. In the universal religion of the New Testament, a sharper division is necessary between the temporal and spiritual spheres, for no nation has any right to break away from the unity of the Church, or to exercise control over matters strictly spiritual.

The priesthood of the Old Testament was more exclusively liturgical than that of the New. The sacrificial system was a complicated one, and the priests were expected to know it. Apart from the liturgy, it does not appear to have been an essential part of their duty to instruct the people ; this rather belonged to the prophets, and later to the scribes. The priesthood therefore was not infallible ; but a right belief was safeguarded by the succession of prophets, an essential feature in the ancient dispensation (Deut. xviii, 15–22). The deposit of faith (to call it by the present technical name) was always open, so that a new doctrine could always be revealed, though the main duty of the prophets was rather to enforce the existing system of faith and morals rather than to introduce anything new. On the other hand the Catholic doctrine is that the deposit of faith, open from the beginning of time, was closed at the end of the apostolic age, so that the business of the Church is not to receive new doctrines, but to teach, to safeguard, to explain, to systematize the old. The gift of infallibility remains, no longer exercised intermittently by prophets, but permanently by the *ecclesia docens*, the teaching Church. More precisely, it is exercised by the Pope when he propounds a doctrine to be held as an article of faith by the whole Church, and by the Catholic episcopacy either in the ordinary discharge of its office, when with the Pope as its head it teaches such a doctrine, or in the extraordinary discharge of its office, when it passes a dogmatic decree in a general council, and the decree receives the Pope's approbation.

The sacraments of the Old Law were of a lesser dignity ; they did not act *ex opere operato*, effecting the grace which they signified, as do those of the New, given the proper dispositions. The sacrificial system (as has been said) was a complicated one. Under the New Law the universal sacrifice prophesied by Malachy (i, 11) is offered in every place without being multiplied, renewing without end the supreme and unique sacrifice of the Suffering Servant of Jehovah (Is. liii), who is the God-Man, our Saviour. Propitiated by this sacrifice, Almighty God dispenses His graces through the seven sacraments, without restricting them thereto.

The former dispensation was temporary and conditional, depending upon the fidelity of the Jews, as is indicated in Deut. xxviii, Jer. xviii, 9–10, the greater part of the Epistle to the Romans, and elsewhere. The Jews rejected their Messiah, and consequently do not hold the place in the new dispensation which was intended for them; there was a violent break, where it was the Lord's will to have rather a gentle development. Rome now stands for what Jerusalem might have been, had it but welcomed the true Light. Nevertheless it remains true that Christ came not to destroy, but to fulfil. For those who have found so much to love and revere in the Old Testament, it is impossible not to share in His grief as He wept over the Holy City and foretold its doom.

The fulfilment of the Old Testament involved greater demands in the spheres both of faith and conduct. Though based upon revelation, the Old Testament did not involve to any large extent the revelation of supernatural mysteries. The New Testament, on the other hand, brought with it the revelation of the greatest of all mysteries, that of the Blessed Trinity, without which indeed the mystery of the Incarnation could hardly have become known. These are the two chief mysteries, and there are a number of secondary mysteries also which find no true counterpart in the Old Testament.

There is also great progress in the ideals of conduct. Speaking generally, the Jew of the Old Testament looked for his reward mainly in this life, as indeed he still does; the New Testament brought with it other-worldly ideals, and therewith (as was to be expected) a more ascetical rule of life. Asceticism we find indeed even in the former Covenant, and chiefly in the practice of fasting; but there is little invitation to leave the world and consecrate one's life to God, either in the solitude of contemplation or in an apostolic career. Our Lord takes the word 'peace,' which in the Old Testament can often be rendered by 'prosperity,' and gives it an utterly unworldly turn, promising a peace which the world cannot give (John xiv, 27); indeed He goes much farther, promising His followers persecution, and bidding them rejoice, and dance for joy, when such persecution takes place, when they are slandered, hated, reviled, cast out (Matt. v, 11 ; Luke vi, 22–23). He was offering a pearl of great price, for which no sacrifice could be too great (Matt. xiii, 45–46). 'If anyone will come after me, let him deny himself, and take up his cross, and follow me. For whosoever would save his life shall lose it ; and whosoever would lose his life for my sake, shall find it ' (Matt. xvi, 24–25). 'Deny himself,' not primarily in the sense of mortification, but in the sense in which Peter 'denied' his Lord (Matt. xxvi, 34) : disown himself, take no account of himself, be dead to himself and living only for Christ.

Nor is man free to decline this sublimer rule of life, at all events in its essential implications. God is not mocked (Gal. vi, 7) : Christ Our Lord, who bids us learn of Him because He is meek and humble of heart, who calls His yoke sweet and His burden light (Matt. xi, 29–30), none the less presses upon man with urgent warnings the peril of eternal damnation, and exhorts him to cut off his foot or pluck out his eye rather than run such a risk (Matt. xviii, 8–9). Thus the great values are all heightened and deepened, and man is raised to a higher plane, in which he must realize his enhanced dignity and importance.

Now all this, it should be carefully observed, presupposes revelation : pre-Mosaic religion, Old Testament religion, New Testament religion, the Catholic religion, all are founded upon revelation. I should like to say, Christian religions in general, and doubtless it would be true of most of their real adherents, and a Catholic need not doubt their purpose and good faith in the matter ; but some Protestant writers have raised such difficulties about the element of revelation that one fears to make too sweeping a statement in the matter. In any case, unless we can be sure of the guarantee of revelation, the Christian faith becomes mere guesswork. Some traditional doctrines, like that of the Blessed Trinity, obviously cannot be known except by revelation, however much some misguided persons may try to deduce such a mystery from religious experience ; apart from revelation, this can only be done by whittling it all away, till little or nothing (we may say roughly) is left of the traditional doctrine. And in any case the virtue of faith, at all events in the traditional sense of believing upon the authority of God Himself, would quite disappear.

Let me again take two examples. I wish to be understood to respect the ability and good faith of any writers whom I mention in this book; if I did not do so, indeed, I should not think them worth mentioning. I could have wished also to treat them at somewhat greater length than is compatible with the limits set for this book. In *Record and Revelation* [1] the Editor, Dr. Wheeler Robinson, has reserved for himself the crucial essay on ' The Philosophy of Revelation.' I do not think that I can be misrepresenting him if I say that his conclusion rules out any certainty that the prophets are proclaiming a truth revealed to them by God. He writes as follows :

' We must not ignore the fact that the divine communication is always coloured by the character and historical conditions of the recipient—in other words that human mediation is always present. Whatever God reveals is revealed as part of the prophet's own consciousness and outlook. The prophet himself might draw an absolute line between the divine oracle and his own reaction to it, but *we* certainly cannot . . . .

' Men may believe or may disbelieve that God of old time spoke unto the fathers in the prophets by divers portions and in divers manners, but what we cannot do is to establish the claim of the prophets on something wholly external to their own activity, whether on a psychical event within or a physical event without. In the last resort, it will be the intrinsic truth of the prophetic utterance, undivorced from its environment, which must establish its authority.' [2]

The limitation is here set upon God Himself; why should He not be able to communicate in various ways with the human spirit, and to make sure that His message is correctly understood and repeated? Why should He not be able to guarantee by a miracle that the message is indeed His? If He could not do so, the greater part of the Old Testament is

[1] *Record and Revelation : Essays on the Old Testament by members of the Society for Old Testament Study.* Oxford, 1938.
[2] Pp. 315-16 : italics in original.

delusion ; but the error lies deeper even than that, for it is based upon an altogether inadequate idea of God Himself.

In the New Testament the main revelation is through Christ ; but nowadays the truth of Christ Himself is called in question. Already in his *Catholicism and Christianity* Dr. Cadoux, for example, had denied Christ's infallibility,[1] and indeed had remarked that ' belief in Jesus ' infallibility and omniscience is . . frankly given up by a large number of Protestant scholars.' He appeals to the ' Inner Light in relation to the historical Jesus,' [2] and indeed devotes the whole of his seventh chapter to ' the ultimacy of the Inner Light,' a thesis which all Catholics must admit if rightly expounded, for all must follow their conscience ; but even a human teacher may rightly demand that statements which his disciples are not in a position to verify be accepted as true, provided that he has proved his knowledge and good faith.

In his later work, *The Historic Mission of Jesus*,[3] he amplifies and emphasizes his position, and states as his conclusion :

' that Jesus' own knowledge was to some extent limited by the conditions of His race and education, that His eschatological teaching contains an element of human ignorance and error, that he uttered predictions which were never fulfilled in the sense in which he uttered them, and that he assumed as true descriptions of the life after death which, resting ultimately on Jewish imagination, cannot rightly be so regarded ' (p. 343).

The question of Christ's eschatology is discussed below at the end of Chapter XI. Dr. Cadoux's other chief difficulty appears to be the eternal punishment of Hell.[4] In regard of both questions Our Lord makes use of that imaginative style which is characteristic of the whole Bible, so that the reader must be careful to distinguish fact and figure. Nevertheless Christ urged the fear of damnation too insistently for His words to be removed from the gospels or explained away. We cannot hope to understand fully the divine purpose, in this or in some other respects ; though indeed in

[1] *Catholicism and Christianity*, p. 215. Allen and Unwin, 1928.
[2] These words are from the ' detailed table of contents,' referring to p. 208.
[3] The Lutterworth Press, 1941.
[4] Cf. *The Historic Mission of Jesus*, pp. 338–45.

the present evils of the world it should be easier to believe in the fitness of a Hell to avenge them. We can at least see how dangerous from every point of view is the error of making little of moral evil, and of reserving one's horror for physical evil, which is often a blessing in disguise, and can always be turned to good by the fervent Christian.

Meanwhile the fundamental question remains, what is the basis of Christianity? For Dr. Cadoux (and of course one is writing, not by way of a personal criticism, but in view of those who may share his views) this basis is his own ' inner light,' since he recognizes the authority neither of the Bible nor of Christ Himself as absolute. We have indeed travelled far when such a position can be regarded either as Protestant or Christian.

In conclusion, it is already obvious, and will appear more fully as we proceed, that Old and New Testament alike are based upon a principle of authority; and therefore this principle is also to be found at work in the Catholic Church. It is indeed essential to any body that professes to have a corporate unity and to teach : much more therefore to a body which claims to possess a truly divine authority both to govern and to teach within its own sphere. Claiming such authority, the Church necessarily claims that nothing can be found in Holy Scripture which contradicts her own mission ; otherwise she would herself be showing a lack of faith in it. False doctrine has usually been accompanied by some perversion of the Scriptures, and her pastors have always claimed authority to resist and correct such perversions.

At the present time, when the attack upon Holy Writ has become so intense as to offer a ' present-day problem,' the Holy See has found it necessary to organize a more thorough teaching and study thereof, and also a more vigilant watch against possible error. This very necessary care in regard to matters biblical is nowadays exercised mainly through the Biblical Commission, whose decrees are not of themselves infallible, though they may be upon other grounds, as when they repeat what is already of faith. They are not issued lightly, and should not be treated lightly ; if, however, a competent Catholic expert, after trying his best to do justice to the arguments for a non-infallible decision, should still find himself unable to agree with it, he must at least abstain respectfully from any propaganda or agitation against it.

Some non-Catholics have attacked this very lack of infallibility, not (so far as one can make out) from any desire of mere truth, but rather from a design to bring infallibility itself to a *reductio ad absurdum*. They ask, why is not everything decided at once infallibly ? The Holy See, however, regards it as a sacred duty not to be prodigal of infallible decrees, but only to issue them when urgently called for, and after long and careful investigation. The mere fact of the privilege and prerogative does not warrant its abuse. Infallibility does not come necessarily from revelation or inspiration or infused knowledge, but from divine assistance which under certain conditions preserves the defining subject (person or persons) from formal error. That divine assistance is divinely promised ; but it has never been understood as absolving the defining subject from the duty of study, research, prayer for light, and consultation. God has promised no miraculous channels by which the defining subject may come to know what is definable truth, or what is the best way or time or form of defining it. The divine assistance which the Church claims is one which is expected to second the efforts of her Head and Pastors in remembering and keeping, expressing and preaching and applying the deposit of truth once delivered.

If the Anglican episcopate or the heads of any other communion ever dared to publish an authoritative definition of a doctrine, biblical or otherwise, they would presumably claim no more than to be issuing a pronouncement of this non-infallible character. The Holy See on its side is slow and sure in its action, yet without forgetting that when the gravity of the occasion demands, a decision can be made that will have a divine guarantee of truth. Nor is it difficult to prove that there *is* such a guarantee, both from Holy Scripture and from tradition.

IV

INSPIRATION

LITTLE has been said so far of the sacred character of Scripture ; nor perhaps for the precise purpose of a work like the present is it quite so important as the historical aspect, by which in large measure the sacred character stands or falls. A total rejection of the historical character of some of the books, and especially of the gospels, would evidently preclude any Catholic view of inspiration, which to a considerable extent is founded upon them. The critical or apologetic study of the gospels proves the divine mission of Christ, who justified His claims by His miracles and by other proofs ; and Christ founded the Church, which in turn teaches the inspiration of the sacred books.

That, at all events, is the simplest and surest line of proof ; though it should be noted that we can deduce much even without invoking the authority of the Church. If once Christ's divine mission be admitted, the significance of His attitude to the Old Testament is at once apparent. Any true prophet might have uttered revealed teaching about the inspiration of a sacred book. And by the admission of Christ's divine mission is not meant the admission that, in the words of the Nicene Creed, He was true God of true God, but only that He was commissioned in an especial way by God to deliver a divine message and carry out a divine work ; in an especial way, inasmuch as it meant the close of the old dispensation and the founding of the new, with differences which have already been summarized. No prophet ever was given a task of such tremendous importance.

There is no sign of any serious controversy between Our

INSPIRATION

Lord and the accepted teachers of the people, the scribes and pharisees, about the authority of the Old Testament: broadly speaking, it was common ground. We find a strong appeal to it in St. Matthew's Gospel, the peculiarly Jewish gospel, both on the part of Our Lord Himself and of the evangelist.[1] It has been calculated by Father Christian Pesch, S.J., that such phrases as, ' it is written,' occur about a hundred and fifty times in the New Testament, and usually as an irrefutable argument.[2] If, then, it be allowed that Christ had this special mission from God, we at once have a strong argument for the inspiration and truth of the Old Testament, an argument strong enough to refute many modern notions upon the subject. But when it has also been shown that He founded an infallible Church, the conclusion admits of no question, and it is further possible to take account of much valuable explanation and development of the doctrine.

With the question of the canon of Scripture it is otherwise. By the canon is meant the list of books recognized as Scripture ; by canonicity we mean, not so much any quality of the book itself, but the fact that it is truly a biblical work. The New Testament itself does not furnish us with a list of the books of the Old Testament, and still less with a list of the books of the New ; moreover, it does not quote the Song of Songs (Canticle of Canticles), and does quote some works which are not canonical, but are attributed to the pagan poets Menander (1 Cor. xv, 33), Epimenides and Aratus (Acts xvii, 28 ; Titus i, 12).

The only way to establish the canon of Scripture is through the teaching of the Church ; and this is in effect what the sixth article of the Thirty-nine Articles of the Church of England does, but it does so after declaring that ' Holy Scripture containeth all things necessary to salvation : so that whatsoever is not read therein, nor may be proved thereby, is not to be required of any man, that it should be believed as an article of the Faith, or be thought requisite

[1] *E.g.*, Matt. xxvi, 54, 56.
[2] *Praelectiones Dogmaticae*, Vol. I, § 606, ed. 3. Herder, 1903.

or necessary to salvation.' The canon of Scripture set forth in the article is certainly 'not read therein, nor may be proved thereby.' Indeed, the article contains another inconsistency, inasmuch as it begins by accepting all those books of Holy Scripture 'of whose authority was never any doubt in the Church,' but ends by stating that 'all the books of the New Testament, as they are commonly received, we do receive, and account them canonical.' Among the books 'commonly received' at the time of the writing of the article were certainly some 'of whose authority' there had been a 'doubt in the Church,' to wit, the Epistle to the Hebrews, 2 Peter, 2-3 John, James, Jude and the Apocalypse.

Nowadays this question of the canon has lost much of its interest, because of the gradual disappearance (still in progress) of any definite notion of inspiration. On the other hand, the Catholic doctrine about inspiration, and about Holy Scripture in general, has undergone a steady development, especially since the appearance of the great biblical encyclical of Pope Leo XIII, the *Providentissimus Deus* (Nov. 18, 1893). In virtue of inspiration God is the primary author of Holy Scripture, the human writer is God's instrument, though still in full use of intellect and will. Almighty God so moves the writer's intellect and will as to produce the work which He desires to have written. Besides these internal motions there is likewise a certain external help ; God sees to it that the writer has proper writing materials, proper leisure, and proper secretaries (if such be used) for the work in hand, and so on. The process of inspiration begins in the writer's mind, but does not reach its term until the whole work has been produced.

Two points should be noticed. In the first place, the Church is not committed to verbal inspiration ; on the contrary, the Holy See may be said rather to favour non-verbal inspiration. But in Catholic study these words mean something different from what they are usually taken to imply outside, where non-verbal inspiration is often intended to imply the abandonment of biblical inerrancy. An example should make the mind of the Biblical Commission clear.

INSPIRATION

On June 27, 1906, it issued some answers expressly allowing the view that while Moses must be recognized as the author of the Pentateuch, he may have committed the actual writing of it to others, after explaining to them his ideas upon the various topics. His own ideas would be inspired, and his final approval of what had been written would likewise be inspired, but the selection of the actual words of the work would not have been made under inspiration. Such an explanation was obviously suggested in order to account for certain differences of style in the Pentateuch, although, as the hypothesis of different sources was explicitly permitted, the explanation is not an indispensable one. Later on (June 24, 1914) the Commission sanctioned (without imposing) a similar solution in regard of the Epistle to the Hebrews, where a similar difficulty of style arises from a comparison with the epistles generally recognized as Pauline. In this latter case the solution comes very near to that of Origen, as quoted by Eusebius in his Church History; nonverbal inspiration as such may be said to have been held explicitly by St. Augustine, and to have been implied by St. Jerome.[1]

[1] Eusebius, *Church History*, Book VI, ch. 25; Augustine, *De Consensu Evangelistarum*, ch. 66, *ad fin.*; Jerome in Gal. i, 11–12; Ep. lvii, 6–10; Ep. cxx, 11.

V

INERRANCY

FROM the fact that the principal author of Holy Writ is God Himself, who can neither deceive nor be deceived, it follows at once that it contains no formal error. It is better to formulate the doctrine in this negative and rather technical way, in order to define it as clearly as possible, in view of the many objections raised against it in our time. It is the traditional Protestant no less than the traditional Catholic view, and may be said to have been an agreed point among the vast majority of Christians until about the beginning of the present century, when the Catholic Church began to find it increasingly necessary to expound and defend her teaching upon the matter. The *Providentissimus Deus*, already mentioned, has proved an important historical land-mark ; it not only contained a clear and vigorous statement of Catholic teaching, but provided a stimulus to Catholic biblical study, which even after half a century is still gathering force rather than losing it.

By formal error is meant error in the objective meaning of the words, the meaning which they are seen in themselves to contain, when full allowance has been made for text and context and all other circumstances. It must be allowed, however, that God as principal author may have inspired a sentence which was only imperfectly understood by the human author, who indeed must often have failed to penetrate the full mind of the Lord. A striking example may be found, not in biblical but in prophetic inspiration, in John xi, 50, which the evangelist declares to have been a prophecy, although Caiaphas can hardly have understood in what

precise sense it was expedient that one man should die for
the people. This is an unique case; but the Epistle to the
Hebrews begins by telling us that God spoke to the prophets
of old (to translate literally) 'in many parts and in many
ways,' and those who knew but a part of the truth could not
expound the whole. To say that Mal. i, 11, for example, is
a prophecy of the Mass is not to say that the prophet foresaw
the Real Presence.

In Holy Scripture as a whole God has likewise expressed
Himself 'in many ways'; nor is it for us to exclude any
way, unless it can be shown to be for some reason unworthy
of Him. The sacred writings are not always precisely what
we might have expected of Him, indeed, it is not difficult
(nor yet, one may hope, irreverent) to imagine various classes
of persons who would have arranged for something quite
different; nevertheless, without claiming any special power
or mandate to justify the ways of God, we can upon serious
reflection come to understand something of the wisdom
underlying them. That, however, is not our immediate
task, which is rather to put forward some general considerations tending to forestall any imputations of formal error.
A sympathetic, not to say docile attitude is a great safeguard
against rash conclusions; in this, as in other matters, a wise
man is quicker to praise than to blame, quicker at the least
to excuse than to condemn.

There is much in Scripture of a very personal nature,
where the sacred writer is describing (for example) his own
emotions; what he writes under the divine impulse of inspiration has divine authority, and is safeguarded from formal
error, but remarks about himself are obviously not remarks
about Almighty God. We may instance the psalmist's
confession of his sins in the *Miserere* (Ps. 51 : Vulg. 50), or
his having his tears for food day and night (Ps. 42 : Vulg. 41).
The inspired author may also confess his ignorance, where
that confession is true, for mere ignorance of itself in no way
implies formal error; St. Paul is not sure whom he has
baptized (1 Cor. i, 16), nor whether he was in or out of the
body in his ecstasies (2 Cor. xii, 2–3).

BACK TO THE BIBLE

Poetry, and poetical language generally, needs careful handling, because it is freer in its use of literary forms. Not merely is it the language of emotion, but of highly imaginative pictures, such as the magnificent portrayal in Ps. 18 (Vg. 17) of Jehovah's descent in His wrath, riding upon a cherub, with smoke pouring forth from His nostrils and flames from His mouth, the storm-cloud His pavilion and the lightning His arrows. In the quaking of the earth, as in the darkening of the sun at the first Pentecost (Acts ii, 20), we have the ' sympathy of nature,' often found also in our English literature, as in Milton's *Lycidas* :

> Rough Satyrs danced, and Fauns with cloven heel
> From the glad sound would not be absent long ;
> And old Damoetas loved to hear our song.

Allegory, too, may be found in Holy Writ, and is the more usual explanation of the Song of Songs (Canticle of Canticles), though evidently some ulterior explications are necessary, for it is admitted that individual details must not always be pressed into some definite application. But in general a spiritual truth is implied, even though it be thought possible to explain the poem without such an implication. After all, the true significance even of the *Spiritual Canticle* of St. John of the Cross, which is modelled upon the Song, would not easily be perceived apart from his own commentary. In English we are familiar with the classical allegories of the *Faerie Queene*, so intricate as to baffle its own author, and of Bunyan's *Pilgrim's Progress*. The latter may illustrate how an allegory may imply formal error ; for to a Catholic the significance of the mean role assigned to the Pope lies chiefly in his being the only representative of anything like the corporate aspect of religion.

Apocalyptic also has its problems, being represented in the Bible chiefly by the Book of Daniel and by the Apocalypse (Revelation), its counterpart in the New Testament. In a certain sense the former has become somewhat easier to interpret nowadays, owing to our better acquaintance with non-biblical examples of the same literary form, of which a

INERRANCY

valuable study has been made by Prof. Székely of Budapest, already well known as the author of a good introduction to Holy Scripture.[1] St. Jerome explains that in the Book of Daniel, Antiochus IV Epiphanes is a first instalment or rehearsal, as it were, of Antichrist, in accordance with the principle of compenetration, which is explained shortly in Chap. X. Almost at the very time that I have been writing this, it has been interesting to read an article in the *Expository Times* for July, 1943, by the Rev. H. V. Martin, M.A., B.D., on Kierkegaard's 'Category of Repetition,' which seems to bear some kinship to this principle : and another article in the corresponding number of the *Hibbert Journal*, which concludes that 'Repetition is, for Kierkegaard, the Christian " frame of reference," by which alone can the man of faith estimate life and thought.' In the Apocalypse we read the curse of God upon the totalitarianism of the Emperor-God, which finds its essential repetition in the dictator of to-day.

Pseudepigraphy, the writing under an assumed name and character, we may pass over lightly, since it is common enough even in modern novels, which no one accuses of falsehood upon this score. St. Jerome and St. Augustine were agreed that Solomon was not the author of the Book of Wisdom, though it is written under his name ; and practically all modern scholars agree with them.

A more difficult problem of literary form may be broached under the rubric *midrash*, a Jewish word of suitable meaning which serves as a more or less technical term for historical fiction. We are familiar with such a literary form in our own literature ; many a novel introduces historical persons or events but weaves round them a tale of fiction. And nobody thinks of calling the authors liars. It may be taken for granted, then, that *midrash* does not of itself involve formal error, and therefore, so far as that goes, it cannot be excluded *a priori* from the Bible, provided that the fiction in question be not unworthy of God on other grounds. In practice the chief objection would arise from the danger of

[1] *Bibliotheca Apocrypha*, Vol. I (Herder, 1913) : *Hermeneutica Biblica Generalis secundum Principia Catholica* (Herder, 1902).

interpreting as fiction what was intended as fact ; this would mean an error of judgment about the literary form.

In the same year (1905) that it gave an answer about historical fiction, the Biblical Commission also dealt with the question of ' implicit quotations.' Is it enough, in dealing with a book of Holy Scripture that appears to narrate historical fact, to say that the writer was merely repeating what he found in his sources, and that nothing more need be asked of him ? In the answer it was required that solid reasons should be given for thinking both that the sacred writer was really quoting another work, and also that he did not intend to make the statement his own. These two answers are explained in more technical Catholic treatises, and it may be enough to point out here that neither historical fiction nor ' implicit quotations ' are ruled out of court *a priori*, but the inerrancy of Holy Scripture is safeguarded by the restrictions put upon the use of such exposition, which had been used too freely. It is worth while also to mention Dr. Bird's edition of Jonah in the Westminster Version, in which the hypothesis is left open of a literary form other than that of strict history, and the articles upon Jonah and Judith in the *Dictionnaire Apologétique*, written upon similar lines by that veteran Old Testament scholar, the late Père Condamin, S.J.

We have recently had offered to us an admirable example of religious ' midrash ' in that striking and even moving work by Miss Dorothy Sayers, *The Man Born to be King* (Gollancz, 1943). Even Archbishop Goodier, in his works upon the life of Our Lord, which have been of so great value to many souls, and are founded upon a deeper knowledge of the evidence than his modest language would perhaps give the reader to suspect, has still followed St. Ignatius' method of meditation in trying to present a concrete picture of the historical scenes, as true as possible to the facts, yet going beyond the strict evidence. ' In many places,' he writes, ' it will be noticed that the author has allowed himself to use his own imagination. Nevertheless, in no instance has he done this without attention to the facts, or without some kind of warrantable evidence.' [1]   Perhaps it is only in the scientific commentaries that the strictest historical method can be followed.

The Bible is certainly intended to convey much historical fact : not according to the method demanded in the scientific study of history to-day, yet without formal error, once allowance has been made for a simpler and more popular manner of narrating, more in keeping with oriental traditions. The Bible likewise has contacts with science in the narrower sense, a sense somewhat unscientifically restricted to the more material side of the universe. Difficulties do arise, though not often ; and it is even more important here than in the case of history to note that the biblical statements are not intended to be scientific in the strict sense of the word.

The *Providentissimus Deus* inculcates mutual respect between scientist and exegete. Each must keep within his own subject. The exegete must be slow to think that a view commonly held by scientists contradicts Scripture, but if he is quite sure that it does, he must reject the view ; views commonly held in this way have come before now to be doubted or rejected. If, on the other hand, the scientist be invading the province of theology or philosophy, as upon occasion he does, he must be dealt with by the experts in those subjects. The language of Sacred Scripture, even when dealing with matters scientific, remains popular in form ; this may sometimes involve speaking of appearances rather than offering scientific explanations. Thus (to apply the doctrine of the encyclical to a well-known passage) in Josh. x, 13, it is said that the sun stood still : details are not supplied such as to enable us to determine with precision what exactly happened, but it would be a sufficient explanation to say that the sun only appeared to stand still. We do not call a man a liar every time he mentions that the sun has risen, although such is not the language of exact science—unless indeed some devotee of Einstein be nowadays prepared to justify it.

[1] *The Public Life of Our Lord Jesus Christ*, Vol. I, pp. xiv–xv. Burns, Oates and Washbourne.

BACK TO THE BIBLE

Something may be expected here upon the early chapters of Genesis, which, however, will be discussed in Part II. For the present it must be enough to insist that it is a cheap solution to endeavour to restrict the truth of Scripture to what directly concerns faith and morals. Almighty God has known from eternity all that scientists will know a century hence, and more besides; and He cannot contradict His own truth, in spite of the misguided efforts of His creatures to make Him do so.

A topic of a rather different kind, which yet should find a place here, is that of morality. The morality of the Bible has often been attacked; but often also the difficulty arises from looking at the matter from a wrong standpoint. Nobody can deny for a moment that evil thoughts, words and deeds are recorded in the Bible; that, however, in itself presents no ground of accusation. Formal error in this case would consist, not in recording, but in inculcating bad morality; for a valid objection, therefore, it would have to be shown both that the act or intention was wrong, and that the Scripture approved of it.

The mere mention of these two conditions is perhaps enough to dispose of a number of passages that might be alleged; still, a considerable number of possible objections remain, for the answer to which we must go to the several commentaries. It must be enough here to make some brief remarks about some well-known incidents. Almighty God, the Creator and Lord of the universe and all mankind, had every right to command the sacrifice of Isaac (Gen. xxii), though He did not allow it to be accomplished. Doubtless it was meant in type; ' for God so loved the world that He gave his only-begotten Son ' (John iii, 16).

About Jacob's statement, ' I am Esau thy firstborn ' (Gen. xxvii, 19), two views have been taken, the one abandoning all defence of it, the other seeking to find in it a deeper truth than lies on the surface. If we take into account, on the one hand, the divine plan which Holy Writ manifests to us, and, on the other hand, the characteristic manner of that manifestation, we may recognize in the sentence a broad truth which is not analysed or accurately defined. Jacob's very name in the Hebrew implied that he was to supplant his elder brother, and it had already been made plain that it was in accord with Jehovah's plan that he should do this (Gen. xxv, 21–26). Isaac, moreover, knew that his blessing was to be ratified (Gen. xxvii, 33, 37). Jacob's sentence therefore may well be taken to express a truth of great historical moment, and to express it in a way which would best sum up the matter for the oriental mind in oriental speech, and indeed for all who can put themselves in sympathy with such mentality.

Jephthah was wicked (or at the best reckless) in his vow, and still more wicked in fulfilling it (Judges xi, 30–31, 39). The psalms pray for the ruin of God's enemies, not merely so far as is necessary for the cause, but as poetic imagination sees it likely or certain to befall in the concrete ; on the other hand, there is no question of the next life. The story of Hosea (Osee) is still more or less under debate. On the one hand, God might foresee unfaithfulness, once again as typical. On the other hand, when we consider such prophetical narratives as Jerem. xxv and Ezek. iv, we may feel the less surprised that there is Catholic support for the opinion that we need not regard the prophecy of Hosea as implying literal fact.

It has seemed necessary to mention a few such difficulties, and to indicate all too briefly some explanations of them, but the reader must beware of thinking that there is little else but difficulties in the Old Testament, and thus of acquiring an utterly wrong perspective ; as a whole it proclaims Almighty God's justice and mercy and truth, and above all His love. 'For whatsoever things were written aforetime were written for our instruction, that through patience and through the comfort of the scriptures we may have hope ' (Rom. xv, 4).

THE Bible does not begin with the story of man, but with the creation of contingent being, and especially of the earth ; and of this wider story it is well to take some account, for it enhances the religious significance of the work. Perhaps it will be more profitable to speak of the end of the world first : the end, that is, so far as man is concerned. Amid all the fairy visions of material progress held out to us, it is well to remember that the earth is gradually (though of course very slowly) becoming uninhabitable. With feverish speed and skill man draws out from it coal and petrol and other important substances ; but the supply is not inexhaustible, and cannot be renewed. And so of other products of the earth. In this connection I may quote some words of the late Dr. Rastall, in an appendix contributed to the Cambridge Summer School book on the Atonement :

' Here we come up against the principle usually formulated as the second law of thermodynamics, or its equivalent, Carnot's principle, which means in plain language that energy is continuously becoming unavailable and that in large quantities. Mathematically the energy is there, but dynamically and mechanically it is of no use for the performance of work, simply because it is too evenly distributed. To express the idea very loosely, energy must be concentrated in lumps and not spread about evenly. All the heat in all the tropical seas of the world will not boil an egg. The nearer it is to a state of equilibrium, the less work can be got out of it ; when a final equilibrium is attained, energy is dead for all practical purposes. . . . It is easy to see what the end must be ; a final equilibrium of the universal world, in which nothing could ever happen, because there are no differences of potential. . . .

' How can this be called evolution ? It is, on the contrary, the negation of it, and the working of evolution in the biological sense must eventually be brought to an end by the opposite inorganic principle of the tendency to physical equilibrium, when life is no longer possible. This dreary prospect is the final goal of the mechanistic and materialistic conception of the universe.' [1]

Professor Whittaker, however, has explained that it seems more likely (still arguing from the purely scientific standpoint) that the world will be destroyed by the heat of the sun :

' There are reasons for believing that at the present time (the sun) is slowly becoming hotter and brighter : and indeed, that before its hydrogen is exhausted, its temperature will have increased to such a degree that terrestrial life as we know it will be impossible. This reverses the expectation, which was generally entertained by past generations of astronomers, that the earth would ultimately become uninhabitable by reason of excessive cold, when the sun's heat had been radiated away : and it brings the end of our world appreciably nearer.' [2]

He also considers that ' there is good evidence for a crisis, happening about 10^9 or 10^{10} years ago, in which the nebulæ, the stars, and even the earth, originated almost simultaneously,' and that to explain this crisis it is simplest ' to postulate a creation *ex nihilo*, an operation of the Divine Will to constitute Nature from nothingness.' [3]

[1] *The Atonement : papers from the Cambridge Summer School of Catholic Studies.* Ed. C. Lattey, S.J., Appendix B; *Evolution in the Physical Universe,* by R. H. Rastall, Sc.D., F.G.S., Fellow of Christ's College, and Lecturer in Economic Geology in the University of Cambridge, pp. 297–8, 301. Burns and Oates, 1928.
[2] *The Beginning and End of the World : Lectures Delivered before the University of Durham.* By E. T. Whittaker, F.R.S., Sc.D., LL.D., Professor of Mathematics in the University of Edinburgh. Oxford University Press, 1942. P. 56.
[3] *Ibid.,* p. 63.

Thus it does not appear to be too much to say that physical science can be found to agree with philosophy in postulating creation, the former arguing from physical facts and the physical laws deducible from them, the latter more abstractly from the evident fact of change and motion and causality, events which cannot go back in an infinite series, for in that case every new change would add, and yet could not add, to the sum total of the changes already befallen.

Thus, not only philosophy, but even physics seem to point back to the beginning of time. It is the first impassable barrier with which the unmitigated evolutionist is confronted. Only an almighty God can bring being out of non-being; even the words ' out of ' in such a sentence are fraught with fallacy, as if non-being were the material out of which could be made being. If we admit the unlimited being and perfection of the Creator, the creature becomes intelligible; otherwise we are landed in a morass of evasions and misconceptions.

From the point of view of physics alone another impassable barrier appears to have been established by the scientists themselves. The older schoolmen were prepared to admit the spontaneous generation of animal life from putrefying matter; but modern science will not allow the production of a living cell from anything but a living cell. How then did life arise? The question is easily answered by those who accept a Creator, for objectively the bestowal of life upon inorganic matter is a lesser thing than creation out of nothing.

Finally comes man; and he is easily distinguished by his powers of intellect and will, pointing to an immaterial soul, such as can only come into being by a direct act of creation. Man can not only recognize a rough kind of triangle in things material, but he can form an accurate concept of a triangle as such, not to be exhausted by any one real or imaginary triangle, but capable of being verified in all such: about this abstract concept of the triangle he can build up a whole series of geometrical propositions, always true wherever the concept of triangle is verified. Or again, man can argue in a syllogism, holding in his mind at one time not only three propositions, but the logical connection between them. Man is a rational animal, John is a man, therefore John is a rational animal. In these and other ways it can be shown that man possesses an immaterial soul : a truth so evident, that some go to the other extreme and deny the existence of things material.

The fact of man's immaterial soul remains true, whether his body be evolved from that of the apes or no. A cumulative argument of wide sweep tends to show that the earliest human bodies resembled more closely those of the apes than the ordinary human body of to-day. This is not altogether astonishing, for the development of the mind tends to react upon the development of the body, and the intellectual descendant of intellectual ancestors is likely to manifest intellectual powers in the very structure of his head. It is peculiar to man among the animals to advance by subduing his environment to himself ; but he appears at the beginning to have lacked all human appliances, and to have been too much occupied with the struggle for existence to have been able to cultivate his mind. For an ample reception of God's gifts and graces it does not seem necessary to suppose that the first man was a kind of super-Aristotle ; even nowadays it is an intense realization of a few truths that makes for sanctity, rather than an elaborate systematization of many. It is the former rather than the latter, for example, that we find in the writings of St. John.

Holy Scripture tells us of the descent of mankind from a single pair, a doctrine closely connected with the doctrine of original sin. It does not appear possible to give a scientific demonstration of this unity of origin ; but neither is it possible to disprove it.[1] It must suffice to know it as revealed truth from Holy Scripture and the teaching of the Church.

The question of the origin of mankind is therefore narrowed

---

[1] Cf. Evolution and Theology, by Dr. Ernest Messenger (Burns and Oates, 1931), s.v. ; Man : Unity of Human Race, in the index. Father Humphrey Johnson, in The Bible and the Early History of Mankind (Burns and Oates, 1943), has discussed ' The Unity of the Human Race ' in an appendix.

down to Adam and Eve. The Biblical Commission (June 30, 1909) has only demanded that ' the special creation of man ' should not be called in question ; and it appears a safe interpretation to refer this special creation to the creation of man's soul. The matter of Adam's body was doubtless created long before his appearance on the earth ; to say that it was created when he first came into being would contradict the text of Genesis itself (Gen. ii, 7). It may be noted that the literal translation of Gen. ii, 7, is : ' God formed the man (*adam*), dust from the ground, '*adamah,* the feminine form of *adam* ; there is a significant play on the words. The Hebrew words need only mean that ' dust from the ground ' was the matter of which Adam was formed, as when God says later (Gen. iii, 19), ' Dust thou art, and unto dust thou shalt return.' It is not necessarily implied in Gen. ii, 7, that there were no intermediate stages between the dust and the body, though it seems more natural to understand this verse and Gen. i, 27, and some other verses in this sense. ' Dust,' of course, must be understood in a large sense. Adam has for his name a word signifying ' man,' just as ' Judah ' could mean either the patriarch Judah or the tribe descended from him : and so of other names. A strong principle of solidarity runs through Holy Scripture.

To a would-be Catholic evolutionist Eve presents rather more of a problem, since the book of Genesis recounts her production in such detail that the Biblical Commission insists on ' the formation of the first woman from the first man,' and so to all appearance does St. Paul (1 Cor. xi, 8). In St. Augustine's view, as Dr. Messenger has shown (*Evolution and Theology*, Pt. IV, chap. 3), the formation of Eve from Adam's rib 'depended upon potencies which could not be actualized in the ordinary course of nature, but only by angelic intervention, acting with God's permission ' (p. 264). To understand this fully we must take into account St. Augustine's doctrine of miracles, carefully explained by Dr. Messenger at the end of his book. Created things have two kinds of ' seminal principles ' (*rationes seminales*) : the one kind are actualized in the ordinary course of nature, the other only under special circumstances. When God brings about these special developments to signify some truth, we have miracles properly so called. Thus Eve would be produced from Adam by the working of natural causes, and yet by a miracle. It must be avowed, however, that St. Augustine's conception of a miracle seems inadequate, and that there appears to be no solid reason for postulating in man such natural powers of generation, even if we suppose the need on their part of a preternatural stimulus. It is best to say simply that Eve was produced by special divine intervention.

VII

PREHISTORY

HISTORY is man's record of his life upon the earth. As the art and science of history has progressed, it has become less content to record merely the actions of man, and has devoted more and more attention to the background of those actions, to the ordinary rather than to the extraordinary features of man's life. This is especially true of the life of prehistoric man, whose culture is of far greater interest even than his movements. We thus come to extend the notion of history even to the succession of events which preceded man's arrival upon this earth, and we speak of the history of the universe, or of this planet.

Still, history in the strict sense remains by common agreement man's story of himself. If, therefore, this chapter is entitled ' Prehistory,' it does not mean that we know nothing at all about early man, but that we know too little to regard it as a real story or record of man. We have a few facts, but even these to a large extent cannot be assigned with certainty to a definite time or place. Biblical history, in particular, can hardly be said to begin before Abraham. It is not worth while to linger upon what may prove a question of words ; it is enough to say that Abraham is the first biblical character of whose life we have a fairly full sketch, which we are also able to relate in a measure to contemporary events.

Up till Abraham, indeed, if not later still, some would be prepared to say that we are dealing with a collection of myths. The Fall, the ages of the patriarchs, the Sons of God, the Flood, the Tower of Babel—all these are said to present a legendary character, which is also emphasized to some extent by our knowledge of some Babylonian parallels, especially in the case of the Flood. In matters of such difficulty and uncertainty it is the policy of this book to suggest possibilities rather than to stake all on a single version of the facts ; and therefore it seems worth while to ask the question, how far would such a myth-explanation be compatible with biblical inspiration and inerrancy ?

Let us try to put such a hypothesis at its best. Many nations, it might be urged, have mythical accounts of their beginnings, of which Virgil's Æneid, for example, is only a comparatively modern and artificial example. Does it seem necessary to hold that they were all supposed to contain nothing but historical facts ? In Virgil's case this is incredible, if we take account of the educated and literary men of his time. To take a big jump back to Homer, it is no less incredible that even the first listeners to some of the tales about the gods took them seriously. And similarly we might argue to the chief Babylonian Flood-story, which in parts runs so closely parallel to that of Genesis. Need it be supposed, then, that Moses, learned in all the wisdom of the Egyptians (Acts vii, 22), was incapable of incorporating such matter into his early narratives, after the manner of other nations, without regarding them as literal history, or expecting his readers to do so ? He would not do so, of course, without some good motive, which it does not seem difficult to imagine : the meditations of the ages upon his writings offer us much profitable thought.

It may be remarked that this is cutting the biblical knot without solving it ; but unless some fatal objection be found to such an explanation, it may be suggested as a possible solution. To hark back to what has been said in Part I on *midrash* as a literary form (pp. 39–41), the Biblical Commission is not irrevocably opposed to this method of interpretation, but rightly requires that solid arguments should be produced to justify it. In this particular case the solid arguments would consist of the serious difficulties of the strictly historical explanation—difficulties which no serious student of the subject is likely to call imaginary—and of the parallels from other literatures which would justify us in any case in speaking of non-historical beginnings as a recognized literary form. Still, as in the case of Jonah in the discussion of *midrash*, there is no intention here of absolutely proving that the non-historical explanation of these early chapters is the right one ; only, if they be accused of formal error, this manner of interpretation must first be shown impossible. And with regard to the Fall, special reservations must be made, based largely on St. Paul.

In the questions now under consideration the consensus of the Fathers of the Church calls for particular attention. Where they agree, they show the authentic Catholic teaching of their time ; but the precise nature of that agreement must be carefully noted. Pope Leo XIII in the *Providentissimus Deus* lays it down that ' their authority is supreme, whensoever they all explain some biblical testimony [1] as belonging to doctrine of faith or morals.' If their authoritiy is to settle the matter, it is not enough that they should all agree in explaining a passage in a particular way, but it must also be plain that they look upon it as a matter of Catholic faith that this explanation should be accepted. Where they do not so regard it, their consensus is sometimes called a merely material, not a formal consensus : or again a merely exegetical, not a dogmatic consensus.

This is important for the matter in hand. It may be said roughly that before the nineteenth century the geographical universality of the Flood and the destruction of nearly all mankind thereby were not called in question by any Catholic ; nevertheless, in 1910 the Capuchin Father Hetzenauer, a distinguished biblical lecturer in Rome, wrote in his commentary on Genesis that the former was ' not probable,' and the latter ' very probable '—not, therefore, certain.[2] He admits that the Fathers agreed in holding both, but denies

---

[1] *i.e.*, a ' testimony ' to a doctrine, a biblical proof of it, taken as such by all the Fathers.

[2] P. Michael Hetzenauer, O.C. : *Commentarius in Librum Genesis : Graecii et Viennae*, 1910, pp. 168, 172. See also the C.T.S. pamphlet, by Father Sutcliffe, S.J., *Who Perished in the Flood ?* (1943).

that they regarded it as a matter of Catholic faith to do so. This is an aspect of the matter that must always be carefully weighed, whether there be question of the Fathers or of the schoolmen or of Catholic tradition generally. It was emphasized, though in other terms, in a letter written in 1906 to a biblical scholar, Bishop Le Camus, by Pope Pius X, the pope who condemned modernism. In praising a work of the bishop's, he says in general that ' while the temerity of those is to be condemned who, conceding more to novelty than to the teaching of the Church, do not hesitate to make use of an over-free method of criticism : so, on the other hand, the attitude of those is not to be approved who dare not break in any respect with the biblical exegesis in vogue up till yesterday, even when, without prejudice to the faith, wise progress in studies invites them bravely to do so.' [1]

If anyone, therefore, be inclined to reject these early chapters of Genesis wholesale, it seems right to ask him whether he can be sure that their literary form does not allow of a larger departure from historical fact than he supposes, and whether he would be prepared to interpret similar narratives in early pagan records on the same strict lines—or, contrariwise, more sympathetically. Nevertheless, the fact must not be disguised that such a freer interpretation has not found much favour in the Catholic Church, and is only put forward here tentatively. And it needs to be balanced by some further remarks upon these chapters, with more attention to a possibly historical exegesis.

Holy Scripture is full of symbolism, the Old Testament perhaps fuller than the New : and the early chapters of Genesis fuller still. If, as suggested in the last chapter, we suppose the first human pair, however privileged by God, not to have attained the full intellectual development of the most cultivated minds of to-day, but rather to have been favoured with an intense grip upon a few momentous truths, then it may have been a help to them, and an additional mercy from their Heavenly Father, that they were granted

[1] I translate from the *Enchiridion Symbolorum*, etc., ed. Denzinger, etc. ; ed. 14–15, p. 519. Herder, 1922.

concrete symbols which would serve to bring home to them
the divine conduct in their regard. Thus, they may not
have been faced from the outset with nothing but abstract
concepts of right and wrong, of obedience and disobedience,
nor yet with nothing but a knowledge of the existence of a
supreme spiritual Being, all-powerful and all-wise. They
hear the sound of Him as He comes, after the fashion of
the East, to walk and talk with them in the cool of the evening
breeze (Gen. iii, 8). Such, doubtless, had been His wont,
to present Himself under a visible appearance, as He did
afterwards to Abraham (Gen. xviii). And He had set two
trees in the garden, and had made their probation a choice
between them, a choice between life and death, between
knowledge of God and knowledge of evil. How tempting
the forbidden fruit to curious woman : how tempting the
wiles of woman to reckless man !

Yet there had been a symbol likewise to warn them.
There is no need to suppose that the serpent which tempted
them had been a dragon upon his legs, any more than to see
in the rainbow the effect of a new law of nature. God had
deigned to be represented in and by human shape, a foreshadowing of the Incarnation ; the serpent, stealthy in
approach and swift in deadly stroke, was to be the symbol for
evermore of ' the ancient serpent, who is the Devil and
Satan ' (Apoc. xx, 2). Even the Babylonian ziggurat, the
' Tower of Babel,' was to bear a message of human pre-
sumption foiled by humiliating helplessness.

The ages of the patriarchs may be taken as schematic
and selective on more grounds than one. We may notice
that there are ten antediluvian patriarchs from Adam to
Noah, both included, and also ten postdiluvian patriarchs
from Shem to Abraham, likewise both included (Gen. v,
xi). The postdiluvian patriarchs have long lives assigned to
them, but are greatly exceeded in this matter by the antediluvian patriarchs, of whom Methuselah reaches the highest
figure, to become famous thereby. Nor is it of much service
to conjecture that the figures were originally smaller, for to
bring them to what would now be regarded as possible

would also be to diminish greatly the antiquity of man,
which even with the larger figures can hardly be taken as a
maximum, having regard to all the evidence in favour of his
much earlier appearance on the earth.   Moreover, the lives
even of the antediluvian patriarchs are short compared to the
reigns of the ten antediluvian kings, according to the Babylonian tradition preserved by Berossus ; these latter total
432,000 years, the shortest reign being for 10,800 years, and
the longest for 64,800. The Babylonian names show a
sufficient connection with the Hebrew ones to convince
Father Hetzenauer, for instance, that the two tables both
come from the same original tradition, preserved pure in
the Hebrew table, corrupted in the Babylonian.[1] It must
be confessed, too, that the lists of Adam's descendants in
chaps. iv and v of Genesis bear a striking resemblance to
each other in several names ; in this case Father Hetzenauer
denies the identity,[2] which, however, would be more easy to
explain if the tables were schematic. He takes ' the sons of
God ' in Gen. vi, 2, to be the descendants of Seth ; the matter
is discussed shortly in Appendix II to vol. IV of the Westminster Version (New Testament), à propos of Jude vi.

[1] *Comm. in Librum Genesis*, pp. 126–7.   [2] *Ibid.*, p. 126.

VIII

THE DOCUMENTARY HYPOTHESIS

THE modern study of the Old Testament outside the Church may be said to be founded upon what is known as the Documentary Hypothesis. It is a theory which is built to a considerable extent upon an analysis of the Pentateuch (*i.e.*, of the first five books of the Bible) into supposed sources ; but the analysis would not of itself be so momentous in its consequences, were it not for the dates assigned to the several sources, and especially to one of them. For these sources are supposed to correspond to the stages of religious evolution to be traced in the historical books other than the Pentateuch, stages which in their turn are supposed to be confirmed by the Pentateuch sources themselves. The whole is a marvellous *tour de force*, depending for the most part upon the Old Testament itself for its justification and evidence, and yet resulting in conclusions which imply that no small portion of the Old Testament is illusion or fraud.

We are bound, therefore, to ask : Is the Old Testament really evidence for this ? Is this the tale it really tells ? Confessions extracted from it under such duress—if extracted they can truly be said to be—must surely be held suspect ? A tremendous amount of scissors-and-paste work is needed to keep the documents of the Documentary Hypothesis in order : little bits of one come butting into another, they get mixed up together, and sometimes nothing short of a strong-minded ' redactor ' can bring order (such as it is) out of the chaos. It needs a ' rainbow ' Bible to give the reader anything like an adequate picture of the jumble which he is expected to find in the Pentateuch. The historical books

escape comparatively lightly, but the prophets are so ruthlessly squared with the theory as to convey the impression
of a vicious circle rather than of a confirmation. And when
we find that revelation and mystery and miracle have been
‘ liquidated ’ in the process, and indeed anything that appears
to require a supernatural explanation—then, perhaps, we may
begin to rub our eyes and fancy that we begin to see day-
light after all. Consciously or unconsciously, the critics
have hardened their minds against anything but a natural-
istic evolution, and are doing the best they can for it under
the circumstances ; but if there is to be any serious discussion of the matter, it must be devoted to the question of
God and religion and other such fundamental matters, rather
than to the exegesis of the Pentateuch. We must put first
things first.

The fact remains that the Documentary Hypothesis is a
very complicated one ; indeed, it would be interesting to know
what percentage of its professed adherents have really thought
it out in all its implications, and have seriously weighed the
pros and cons of the case. It may serve to simplify matters
somewhat if in the following discussion Wellhausen’s *Prolegomena to the History of Israel* [1] be kept chiefly (though not
exclusively) in view. He was the chief popularizer of the
Documentary Hypothesis, which does not seem to have
changed its shape much since his time. It is, of course, impossible to criticize this work and its presuppositions ex-
haustively ; it must be enough to consider rather briefly a
few of the more vital points. This, at least, in a work like
the present is indispensable.

Four main sources are assigned to the Pentateuch, and
to the book of Joshua which follows it : they are represented
by J (Jahvistic or Yahwistic source), E (Elohistic source),
D (mainly Deuteronomy) and P (the ‘ Priestly Code ’). It
was the view propounded by Reuss in the last century that
P was not (as hitherto supposed) the most ancient of the
sources, but the most recent, that marked the final passage
into evolutionary rationalism ; it is now dated to the Baby-

[1] English translation by Black and Menzies. A. and C. Black, 1885.

lonian exile (in the sixth century B.C.) or later still. The enormous significance of this lies in the fact that to this source is assigned (to speak rather roughly) all that belongs to systematic religion. It is a secondary matter, not further to be touched on here, that much of what belongs to organized nationality is likewise attributed to it.

The distinction between J and E does not greatly matter, although the emphasis laid on the distinction of the divine names (to which we shall shortly return) is not justified. These two sources are supposed to be the earliest. Nor does the source D as such concern us to any great extent. Deuteronomy is before all else a series of discourses, and therefore may well be using a more rhetorical style, such as would entail a rather different vocabulary. It offers parallel versions of some of the laws, such as may have existed in Hebrew tradition before the Exodus. But the so-called ' Priestly Code ' is said to comprise all that belongs to a definite subject-matter, and the argument from vocabulary, precisely to prove that it *is* a distinct source, is largely fallacious. In the history of almost any war which had a naval side to it, this side of it might possibly be written by a specially selected naval expert, but the use of special terms would go no way at all to prove distinct authorship, because the subject-matter itself would require such special terms. And the use of such terms might almost insensibly have some effect on the rest of the vocabulary, leading to the introduction of other terms which for some reason or other might seem to suit better the definitely naval terms. So it is with the ' Priestly Code ' ; supposing (as it seems right to suppose) that the original writer regarded its subject-matter as an integral part of his narrative, it would not be surprising to find him slipping into a rather different vocabulary when he came to deal with it.

The use of the divine names was the criterion originally used by Astruc in the eighteenth century as the criterion of Pentateuch sources, and it has always played a considerable part in this matter, though in modern times the ' critics ' have shown themselves rather shy of stressing it. It seems worth while to say a little about this criterion before passing to more directly historical issues. It should be explained that the letter J itself stands for Jahveh or (in its least accurate but more literary form) Jehovah, the proper name of God, now usually written Yahweh. The Jews would not pronounce this sacred name, and so (according to their usual practice) they placed under its letters the vowel-points of the word they did read, Adonay (properly, ' my Lord ') ; it was misunderstanding of this proceeding that gave rise to the name ' Jehovah,' which is thus really composed of the letters of one word and the vowel-points of another. The older versions followed the Jewish practice of reading ' Lord ' where the original Hebrew text had Yahweh, which latter word accordingly does not appear in them. J, however, is intended to stand for the parts of the Pentateuch using the divine name Jahveh (apart from its use in D and P, which cannot here be discussed) ; and E for the parts using the name Elohim, the ordinary Hebrew name for God, though as a matter of fact it is not used exclusively of God. The two parts are thus attributed to two distinct sources.

As a criterion of sources the use of the divine names works awkwardly, as the late Harold Wiener, for example, has shown.[1] At the very outset of the book of Genesis we are bidden see two alternative stories of creation, which it may be worth while to discuss shortly from this and other points of view. The first point we notice is that the division between the supposed two creations occurs in the middle of a sentence, the second part of which (Gen. ii, 4b), assigned with what follows to J, had to wait a few centuries for its subject and verb in Gen. ii, 4a, assigned with what precedes to P. Or are we to say that Gen. ii, 4b, otherwise so long left high and dry, was added later to make a better join between P and J ? If so, it is clearer than ever that what follows is not really a second creation at all, but merely sets the scene for the story of the Fall. Then again, why should the

[1] *E.g.*, in *Essays in Pentateuchal Criticism,* Elliot Stock (1910), ch. I. In this and other books Wiener has at times criticized the critics with considerable effect.

earlier part be assigned to P? Its peculiar rhythmical arrangement and repeated formulae differ from anything found in the rest of P or even, one might well say, in the rest of the Bible. To speak of the rest of P as ' homogeneous in style and character with Gen. i, 1–ii, 4a,' [1] is to betray surprising literary obtuseness. Surely, if style is to go for anything, it must be regarded as unique, a magnificent preface— one is almost inclined to call it a solemn prefatory chant—to the whole Pentateuch, or to the whole of the Scriptures.

And the divine names? Elohim alone is used in Gen. i, 1– ii, 4a, after which Yahweh appears. But Elohim also appears by itself in Gen. iii, 1, 3, 4; and a further complication is to be found in the fact that the combination Yahweh Elohim (' the Lord God '), found so often in Gen. ii, 4b–iii, 23, is found but rarely in the rest of the Old Testament, and in the Pentateuch only in Exod. ix, 30, where it is naturally suspect, especially as there is also some textual evidence against it. So far as the text of the divine names goes, therefore, we have in Gen. ii, 4b–iii, 24, another unique passage ; but what with the repeated occurrence of Yahweh Elohim, the occurrence of Elohim by itself, the non-occurrence of Yahweh by itself, and finally the textual evidence against the addition of Yahweh in Gen. ii, 9, 21, it seems a fairly safe conclusion that Yahweh ought to disappear from Gen. ii, 4b–iii, 23. A textual note on Gen. ii, 4, in the Kittel edition of the Hebrew Old Testament asserts that Elohim or *rather* Yahweh from Gen. ii, 4b to Gen. iii, 23 seems to be an editorial addition, adding that the Greek Old Testament in the usual (' Septuagint ') text and the Old Latin (*i.e.*, pre-Jerome) Old Testament often read Elohim alone.

Thus, the whole argument from the divine names for the division of Gen. i–iii into P and J may be said to disappear. It has seemed worth while to make this clear, because, in spite of deprecatory remarks made nowadays as the weakness of the argument from the divine names becomes more apparent, greater weight still seems to be attached to them than to any other single word or phrase.

[1] *The Book of Genesis*, ed. S. R. Driver, ed. 9, p. iv. Methuen, 1913.

THE DOCUMENTARY HYPOTHESIS

It should be added for the sake of completeness that there are also other reasons for suspecting later changes of the divine names, which thus tend to weaken any argument derived from them. It may be enough to quote another short passage from S. R. Driver's *Book of Genesis* (p. 407) : by ' the Chronicler ' is meant the author of Chronicles (Paralipomena) i–ii :

' The Chronicler . . . is apt to show a preference for *Elohim* (though he also uses *Yahweh*), and sometimes changes *Yahweh* of his source into *Elohim* ; and the exceptional preponderance of *Elohim* in Book II of the Psalms, and in Psalms 73–83, as compared with the rest of the Psalter, shows that here the editor, or collector, must have substituted it for an original *Yahweh*.'

Some references are omitted from this quotation, but the reader will understand sufficiently what is meant by comparing Ps. xiv (xiii) with Ps. liii (lii), remembering that ' Lord ' stands for Yahweh. If, then, the divine names were liable to be changed in the psalms and Chronicles, how can we be sure that they have not been changed in the Pentateuch, even in other places? As S. R. Driver practically admits,[1] it is not usually to be expected that the change should be obvious.

It should be explained in conclusion that while it has seemed worth while to dwell on one weak point in the usual documentary division, there is no intention here of attacking all distinction of sources. To the present writer the seizure and sale of Joseph (Gen. xxxvii) has always seemed to offer a strong case for such distinction ; and Gen. xiv seems unique in its general character. Since, as has been noted earlier in this chapter, it is the date of the ' Priestly Code ' that is of primary importance, it is worth noting that S. R. Driver, after carefully splitting up the Flood story into its J and P sections, fails to observe that the same division should also be introduced into the ancient Babylonian Gilgamesh epic, which runs parallel to it, and which he proceeds to quote at some length, and to date (at the least) to 2200 B.C.

[1] *The Book of Genesis*, Addenda II, pp. XLV–XLVI.

IX

WELLHAUSEN'S HISTORICAL STAGES

In the last chapter some criticism has been offered of the Documentary Hypothesis upon its literary side ; but, as was pointed out at the beginning of the chapter, it is not really the fact or fiction of sources that matters so much as the dates assigned to them, and more especially the date assigned to P. The Biblical Commission, in particular, while insisting on the Mosaic authorship of the Pentateuch, saw no difficulty in admitting that Moses might have used written or oral sources (June 27, 1906). In Wellhausen's hypothesis, accordingly, the late dating of the ' Priestly Code ' is based in the main, not upon literary arguments as such, but upon an interpretation of the religious development of the Hebrews founded to a large extent upon books other than the Pentateuch. The Pentateuch sources then come in to confirm the argument, corresponding, according to him, to the several stages already detected elsewhere.

' My whole position is contained in my first chapter,' he writes (*Prolegomena*, p. 368) : the which chapter it will therefore be worth while to consider rather carefully, much as in the last chapter we considered the alleged sources of Gen. i–iii. Considerations of space forbid more. The chapter is entitled, ' The Place of Worship,' and with that we may begin. The general contention here is that there is no justification for so completely upsetting the biblical story as it will be seen that Wellhausen does. He professes to distinguish in the historical and prophetical books three main stages in the history of ' The Place of Worship ' ; and then to find in the Pentateuchal sources three corresponding stages (J–E, D, P)

in the regulations dealing with the subject. It is his contention that these regulations are not really of Mosaic origin,
but belong to, and in a measure helped to produce, the
historical stages to which they correspond. The argument
is an intricate one, a fact to which it may owe something of
its vogue, for it is a still more intricate business to counter it.
In order to help the reader to follow the whole argument
more easily, its main divisions will be indicated by headings
at the beginnings of the paragraphs. By the 'historical'
stages are here meant the stages as supposed to appear in
the historical and prophetical books; the books recognized
to be in the main historical are Judges, 1-2 Samuel, 1-2 Kings.
The last four are also reckoned as 1-4 Kings in the Vulgate.
By the 'documentary' stages are here meant the same
stages as supposed to appear in the supposed Pentateuchal
sources. W. henceforth stands for Wellhausen, and the
page references occasionally given are to the English translation of his *Prolegomena*.

First historical stage according to W.—There is no sign in
Hebrew antiquity of a sanctuary of exclusive legitimacy.
Anybody might sacrifice anywhere, and every slaughter of
an animal was a sacrifice. In Judges and Samuel hardly a
place is mentioned without also mention of altar and sacrifice.
After Solomon no king is left uncensured for having tolerated
the high places; but Solomon himself sacrifices at Gibeon
(1 Kings iii, 4) and Samuel at Bethlehem (1 Sam. xvi, 5).
For Israel as a whole, Jerusalem was never the place which
Jehovah had chosen, and least of all after the division of the
kingdom. The tribe of Ephraim worshipped Jehovah at
Bethel and Dan, Shechem and Samaria, Penuel and Mizpah,
and at many other places. 'Nobody had the faintest
suspicion that such conduct was heretical and forbidden'
(pp. 21–22).

Three criticisms of first historical stage.—(1) W. himself
explains matters. 'Not until the house had been built to
the name of Jehovah—such is the idea—did the law come
into force which forbade having other places of worship
besides' (p. 19). And he very appositely quotes 1 Kings iii,

2 : ' The people sacrificed upon the high places, for as yet no house to the name of Jehovah had been built.' But this is the principle recognized likewise in the Pentateuch. Of the *intermediate* period we read in Exod. xx, 24 (assigned to J) : ' An altar of earth thou shalt make unto me, and shalt sacrifice thereon thy burnt offerings . . . in every place where I cause my name to be remembered I will come unto thee and I will bless thee.' Thus any kind of divine manifestation would for the time being warrants sacrifice. But, in accord with 1 Kings iii, 2, once Jerusalem was occupied and the Temple built, Deut. xii. 13–14 (D) ruled that the latter is to be the exclusive place of worship : ' Take heed to thyself that thou offer not thy burnt offerings in every place that thou seest ; but in the place which the Lord shall choose in one of thy tribes, there thou shalt offer thy burnt offerings, and there thou shalt do all that I command thee.' Thus, so far as the question of the centralization of worship goes, principle and practice agree in the historical and prophetical books on the one hand, and the Pentateuch on the other.

(2) To judge from the way in which W. writes, one would think that it was merely a question whether Jehovah was to be worshipped in one place or several. In fact, however, the high places had early—in some cases from the beginning— been contaminated with idolatry, so that their ultimate abolition had a totally different import from that imagined by W. The present writer has had to protest against a similar misconception elsewhere : [1] some of the passages whereby a proof is attempted that the prophets were hostile to all sacrifice are clearly concerned with idolatry, to which of course they would in any case be opposed. Passages which illustrate the practice of idolatry at the high places are : 1 Kings xii, 25–33 ; xiii, 33–34 ; 2 Kings xvii, 7–17 ; xxii, 17 ; xxiii, 5–6, 10–15.

(3) Lastly, W. cannot be right in supposing that in primitive days every slaughter was a sacrifice. That this was not the case *before* Moses, which is the main point, is clear from

[1] *The Journal of Theological Studies*, Vol. 42, pp. 155–65 (July–October, 1941) : *The Prophets and Sacrifice : a study in Biblical Relativity.*

such passages as Gen. xviii. 7; xxvii, 9–14. That it was not the case *after* Moses is no less clear from Deut. xii, 15. Curiously enough, the one passage which at first sight supports W.'s view is in Lev. xvii, 3–4, assigned to P : no animal may be killed that is not sacrificed before Jehovah's tabernacle. Now it is so incredible that such a regulation was introduced after the exile (the date assigned to P), only to disappear in a short time without further trace either of appearance or disappearance, that this passage tells against the 'critical' view itself of P. The true explanation of it appears to be that it was an obvious and easy precaution against idolatry in the desert, impossible of execution either before or afterwards, and only intended to be temporary. Otherwise it would conflict with Deut. xii, 15, which allowed all necessary latitude for mere killing.

Second historical stage according to W.—The main features are the prophets' attacks upon the high places, the fall of Samaria, and the reform of Josiah. A multitude of sanctuaries is presupposed, at which Jehovah is served in good faith. It was something quite new when the prophets Amos and Hosea began to declare that Gilgal and Bethel and Beersheba were an abomination to Him : not (according to W.) that they objected to the high places themselves, but only to the abuses of the cults there carried on, and to the false value attached to them. What actually happened was that the high place at Jerusalem ultimately abolished all the others ; it had always dominated Judah, and with the fall of Samaria (721 B.C.) there was no serious rival in the northern kingdom. This fall was looked upon as a divine punishment ; even before this the prophets had been inclined to favour Jerusalem (*e.g.*, Amos i, 2), and now they looked upon the deliverance of Jerusalem from Sennacherib (Is. xxxvii) as a sign of divine protection.

About King Hezekiah's removal of the high places (2 Kings xviii, 4), it suits W. to be sceptical (p. 25), for it does not offer the same easy equation with Deuteronomy as the high priest Hilkiah's finding of the book in 621 B.C., the contents of which are confirmed by the prophetess Huldah (2 Kings xxii).

King Josiah's vigorous action on the strength of this is
described in 2 Kings xxiii. ' Yet what a vitality did the green
trees upon the high mountains still continue to show ! Even
now they were but polled, not uprooted ' (p. 27).

Criticism of second historical stage.—In the first place,
attention must be called once again to the way in which W.
passes over in silence all indications of idolatry ; enough has
been said about this in the second criticism on the first historical stage. In Old Testament history, and especially in
pre-exilic history, the fact or danger of idolatry must never
be lost sight of. Certainly the prophets never lost sight of it.
The language of Amos and Hosea, according to W., ' was
one hitherto unheard of ' (p. 23)—yes, but on W.'s theory,
theirs is the earliest evidence available, and for any previous
state of affairs we have only his own *ipse dixit*. Once the
prophets *are* there to speak, W. admits that they are far from
taking his view of the matter ; they attack the high places,
they see in the destruction of Samaria a divine punishment,
they favour Jerusalem ! Take the biblical story at its face-
value, without any regard for all these ' critical ' attempts to
turn it upside down, and this is just what we should expect.
As for Josiah's reform, it is treated by W. and others as a
fraud ; ' the book of the law ' (2 Kings xxii, 8) was written
to be discovered. To this we shall return.

Third historical stage according to W.—Without the Babylonian exile (586–538 B.C.) King Josiah's reform would not
have succeeded. The exile caused a great breach of con-
tinuity in the national history. ' From the exile there
returned, not the nation, but a religious sect—those, namely,
who had given themselves up body and soul to the reforma-
tion ideas ' (p. 28). They settled round about Jerusalem,
and never dreamt of restoring the cults on the high places.

Criticism of third historical stage.—There is a good deal of
truth in the picture here presented ; it is enough to say that
the language is exaggerated. We turn now to the documentary sources, which are supposed to correspond to these
historical stages. In the light of what has already been
written they admit of more summary treatment.

First documentary stage according to W.—The sources J–E sanction a multiplicity of altars, on sites not arbitrarily chosen, but connected with some divine manifestation (pp. 29–30).

Criticism of same.—Something has already been written about this in the first criticism of the first historical stage ; the above statement as it stands is true, but it in no way contradicts what is so often stated or implied elsewhere in the Old Testament, the position of the ark of the covenant as the official centre of the cult. It was not at first the only lawful place of sacrifice.

Second documentary stage according to W.—' Deuteronomy (D) demands local unity of worship '(Contents, p. xi). To this proposition is added another of great importance : not merely that the book found by Hilkiah in 621 B.C. was Deuteronomy, as explained above, but that the book had just been written (though in a shorter form, a minor point not worth discussing here). Although W. does not say so explicitly, it is an easy conclusion from his words on p. 34 that the ' finding ' of the book was no accident.

Criticism of same.—The demand for unity of worship in Deuteronomy has been sufficiently discussed above, in the first criticism of the first historical stage ; the unity of worship prescribed in the Pentateuch had reference to the future. We have already seen there that W. himself (perhaps without realizing the full significance of the admission) points out that the same principle is recognized in 1 Kings iii, 2. Full centralization was only to come with the building of the Temple.

But why should the composition of Deuteronomy be put so late as 621 B.C. ? Why should W. be so credulous about King Josiah's proceedings in 2 Kings xxii, and so sceptical about King Hezekiah's in 2 Kings xviii ? He writes of Deuteronomy as ' a law so living, which stands at every point in immediate contact with reality, which is at war with traditionary custom ' (p. 34) ; but this ' traditionary custom ' was not immediately abolished by Deuteronomy, except on W.'s hypothesis that the book was a fraud, unjustifiably referred back to Moses. It is marked by a certain vigour, because it contains Moses' last instructions, preceding the entry of the Hebrews into the promised land ; naturally he insists upon the Temple worship to be instituted there, a glorious, permanent, exclusive centre of religion for the nation in the land now to be given it. For Hilkiah, the book which he has found is ' the book of the Law ' (2 Kings xxii, 8), as it is likewise for King Josiah (2 Kings xxiii, 24), who indeed ' turned to Jehovah with all his heart, and with all his soul, and with all his might, according to all the Law of Moses ' (2 Kings xxiii, 25). It is unlikely that he would have taken such strong measures without first satisfying himself that it really *was* the law of Moses. For W., the Old Testament is largely a history of unscrupulous fraud and unlimited gullibility. Once we accept belief in a living God, with all its implications, the sacred story is more credible as it stands. If we wish to know how ' the book of the Law ' ever came to be lost, we have only to read 2 Kings xxi ; in those days there cannot have been so many copies of it, and in the two reigns preceding that of Josiah even the Temple was not a safe place for it. That only Deuteronomy is meant by ' the book of the Law ' is possibly true, but it remains an unproved and unprovable assumption.

Third documentary stage according to W.—The ' Priestly Code ' (now called P, though W. called it RQ) presupposes the unity commanded by Deuteronomy, and transfers it, by means of the tabernacle, to primitive times. We have in P not merely narrative, but law : it expresses the law of Deuteronomy in terms of history, as though it had always been in force. ' For the truth is, that the tabernacle is the copy, not the prototype, of the temple at Jerusalem ' (p. 37).

Criticism of same.—This is evidently intended to be the death-stroke of the traditional view of Old Testament worship, and indeed of the Pentateuchal account itself ; but it is marked by an *ignoratio elenchi*—a missing of the point—so complete and so astonishing that it seems incredible that an intelligent and unbiased reader of the Old Testament should fall into such a blunder. The centre of worship was not, as

W. supposes, the tabernacle, but the ark of the covenant inside it, with the 'mercy-seat' or 'propitiatory' over the ark, whence Jehovah Himself was to speak (Exod. xxv, 22). Seldom (if the phrase may be applied reverently) has there been such a clear case of the husk being mistaken for the kernel.

W. writes with some exaggeration that the whole history of the ark ' down to the period of its being deposited in the temple of Solomon is a proof that it was regarded as quite independent of any tent specially consecrated for its reception ' (p. 41). Coming then to the Mosaic tabernacle, the tabernacle according to P, he tries to heighten the contrast by still more exaggeration, insisting on the dependence of the ark on the tabernacle more than the evidence warrants. 'According to the law,' he writes, ' the two things,' ark and tabernacle, ' belong necessarily to each other ; the one cannot exist without the other ; both are of equally great importance. The tabernacle must everywhere accompany the symbol of its presence ; the darkness of the holy of holies is at the same time the life-element of the ark ; only under compulsion of necessity, and even then not except under the covering of the curtains, does it leave its lodging during a march, only to return to it again as soon as the new halting-place is reached ' (pp. 41–42).

Now to call the ark the symbol of the presence of the tabernacle is sheer nonsense, and there is nothing more to be said about it ; but even the rest of this quotation, the ' life-element,' the ' compulsion of necessity,' is Wellhausen, not Moses or the Pentateuch. At the outset the ark is made portable, and portable it remains, with the Levites for porters (cf. Numb. iv ; etc.) ; and of course it could not travel under the shelter of the tabernacle. When King David left Jerusalem in flight from Absalom, it was taken for granted that the ark must travel once more ; but David would not have it so (2 Sam. xv, 24–25). So it had been done with Saul (1 Sam. xiv, 18), and in the days of Heli (1 Sam. iv). No doubt it was the loss of the ark and the sack of Shiloh (cf. Jos. xviii, 1 : 1 Sam. i–iv : Jerem. vii, 12–14) that led to a permanent separation of ark and tabernacle ; but the sacred writer's

BACK TO THE BIBLE

interest remains with the former, which remains at Kiriath-
jearim for twenty years (1 Sam. vii, 1–2), until David brings
it to Jerusalem to await the building of the Temple (2 Sam.
vi). Thus there is nothing difficult or mysterious about the
history of the ark, in spite of W.'s forced antithesis between
the Mosaic and the historic ark, based upon an exaggerated
view of the importance of the tabernacle.

Yet it is upon this forced antithesis that W.'s position
really depends ; it is to this that his first chapter leads up,
and it is his own statement that ' my whole position is contained in my first chapter ' (*Prolegomena*, p. 368). It is thus
a position built on sand. And in this matter of the cult, too,
as at the end of the previous chapter, we can produce a
parallel in non-biblical sources which makes for an early date.
Dr. Jack, in his study of the ancient tablets found at Ras
Shamra on the Syrian coast,[1] dates them from 1470 B.C.
to 1366 B.C., and shows how much of the ' Priestly Code '
had been anticipated in the ancestral religion of the Phoeni-
cians.

[1] *The Ras Shamra Tablets : Their Bearing on the Old Testament.* T. and
T. Clark, 1935.

X

THE PROPHETS

THE Jewish state was in principle a theocracy, so that the nation acquiesced but uneasily in foreign rule even of the better kind, though recognizing among its heroes some who had distinguished themselves under foreign rulers, such as Joseph and Daniel. The theocracy, the rule of God, implied divine origin, divine guidance, divine government; and these again implied revelation. The third chapter of this work is largely concerned with revelation; but at this stage it is necessary to insist once again upon the crucial character of this issue for the study of the Old Testament. It is possible to study fruitfully some departments of history without bestowing serious attention upon the question of revelation, or even of religion in general; but in treating of the Old Testament it is absurd to attempt such a task. Speaking broadly, either there was continual divine intervention, or else there was continual fraud or delusion, or both together. It is not enough, for example, to attribute 'insight' to the true prophets, and the lack of it to the false prophets; true and false prophets alike regarded it as essential to the office that they should have a genuine revelation, and both claimed to have had it. Many miracles are recounted; so that upon this score also considerable parts of the Old Testament must be adjudged merely pious (or impious) fiction, if miracles are to be absolutely ruled out of court. The crucial question, as has been said in chapter II, is that of God; nevertheless, the issue can also be considered *a posteriori*, for presuppositions stand self-condemned which involve such a flouting of the historical evidence.

BACK TO THE BIBLE

A prophet seems best defined as one who has received a revelation and a mission from God; not merely is some truth conveyed to him by God, but he is charged to deliver it to some person or persons, usually the Hebrews. So we read in the case of the greater prophets (Isaiah vi; Jerem. i; Ezek. ii); but a revelation and a mission are really implied every time the formula is used, 'Thus saith Jehovah,' or its equivalents. The prophets need not write: Elijah does not appear to have done so, though, upon the other hand, the writings of others have been lost, such as those of Nathan and Gad (I Chron. xxix, 29). In Deut. xviii, 18–22, prophecy is promised as a permanent institution in Israel, though the New Testament shows that the passage found its supreme fulfilment in Christ. The one guarantee there offered is that the prophet is a false one whose prediction does not come to pass; but evidently miracles and the fulfilment of predictions might be positive proof of the true prophet. Miracles and prophecies have in truth never ceased, though with the close of the apostolic age prophets have not the same public office as before, and therefore are not usually called by that name; still, more is often known about the saints who have prophesied than about the Old Testament prophets, so that they offer a valuable study even for strictly biblical purposes, and to neglect their experiences is not scientific.

It has' been said above that a prophet must have received revelation and mission; he is charged with a message to others. This seems to be the Old Testament concept of a prophet; though it must be remembered that in the Old Testament theocracy the scope of prophecy went far beyond what we should nowadays regard as belonging to faith and morals. Isaiah, for example, warned the Hebrews against relying upon help from Egypt (Isaiah xxx, 1–5 : xxxi, 1–3); Jeremiah counselled submission to Babylon (Jerem. xxvii). But if we accept this definition of a prophet, it must be admitted that both in Old and New Testament some have received revelation without mission, who should not therefore be given the title. This is true in the main of the patriarchs who received divine communications; for as a rule there is little sign that they were charged to repeat them to others. The same holds good of many Christian mystics, whose revelations have been given them mainly for their own benefit; many have been charged with a commission for others, but a commission not bearing the public and official character of the prophets of the Old Covenant.

The Jewish state, as has been said above, was in principle a theocracy; and therefore it was fitting that its chief founders should act under revelation and deserve the title of prophet, though it is not often given them. Moses, the human founder of the Law, was a prophet in a unique sense, and it must not be inferred from Deut. xviii, 18, that the prophets who followed him were on a level with him, until we come to New Testament times, to the Baptist and to Christ Himself. Jehovah places Moses far above the ordinary prophet:

> With my servant Moses it is not so:
> In all my household he is the faithful one:
> Face to face I speak with him,
> In person and not in dark sayings:
> And Jehovah's form he beholdeth (Num. xii, 7–8).

The mission of Moses was unique, like his revelation, since it embraced not only the deliverance from Egypt, but the foundation of the Hebrew religion as an organized system. His successor Joshua was likewise a prophet, and could preface a discourse with the formula so common later, ' Thus saith Jehovah ' (Josh. xxiv, 2). Samuel, the last and greatest of the judges, was also one of the greatest of the prophets; his story is one of singular beauty and interest. It seems highly probable that King David was favoured, not merely with inspiration, but with revelation, yet there is a curious absence of any positive proof of this; we read only that he received answers through the ephod (1 Sam. xxiii, 9 : xxx, 7) and messages through the prophets. Of Solomon, however, we have recorded both revelation (*cf.* 1 Kings xi, 9–13) and inspiration. After him the divine guidance of the rulers appears to be only indirect, through the prophets and the sacred writings.

The work of the prophets, however, and likewise the revelations of the patriarchs, were not limited to the immediate future, but foreshadowed a greater dispensation to come. To several among them it was made clear that God's kingdom was to come upon earth in a more developed form ; they did not themselves receive the promises, but greeted them from afar. It is impossible in this place to review at all fully the great converging argument which convinced the Jews that a Messiah was to come to them ; when their expectation was at its height, He actually came. Like all the prophets, He called to repentance rather than to revolt ; and He attacked vehemently the crabbed elaborating of minute details which hid from view the weighty things of the Law. The traditions of men which made void the law of God are written deep in the rabbinical literature, which affords such a contrast to the New Testament and the writings of the great Catholic doctors and saints.

' My kingdom is not of this world ' (John xviii, 36). It was to be a kingdom ; Christ chose to be sentenced to death for His kingship rather than repudiate it. It was to be otherworldly ; Pilate saw plainly that it did not mean revolt from Rome, but in the face of Jewish opposition he feared to acquit one who still would not renounce His claim to be a king. Not long before, in fact, in His picture of the last judgment, Christ had evidently referred to Himself as ' the King ' (Matt. xxv, 34, 40).

Still, we must not lightly brush aside all the promises of temporal bliss in the Old Testament, especially when we remember at how late a stage the belief in the rewards and punishments of the next life took clear shape in the Book of Wisdom. ' Hadst *thou* but known ! ' (Luke xix, 42). If the Jewish nation had acknowledged Christ for its Messiah, it would have had a very different future ; we can imagine the new theocracy, like the old, being ruled from Jerusalem, with Palestine the papal state, and a very different destiny allotted to it. What has actually happened, we may say in a certain sense and with due reverence, is God's second-best ; it was the thought of a far better dispensation for the chosen race that drew tears from Messiah now come, about to enter His own city in a triumph that was to prove so short and hollow. Nevertheless, the main features of the new theocracy were not to be sacrificed; it was to be universal, other-worldly, intensely one: a perfect society, subject to none other, with priestly power of sacrament and sacrifice, infallible in truth.

The promises were conditional, as we see clearly enough from the end of Deuteronomy (Deut. xxviii), reinforced by the strong words of Jeremiah (Jerem. xviii, 7–10), and some other passages. St. Paul likewise, as was necessary to his purpose, grapples with the whole problem in the Epistle to the Romans (Rom. ix–xi). It would take too long to explain fully his somewhat intricate discussion of the issue, which may be summarized as follows. God could and did reject the Jews; but the Apostle goes on to show that they had merited such rejection, thus himself also implying a condition in the Old Testament promises. Nevertheless, he contributes something fresh to the discussion in the limitations he sets forth to this rejection. They are not wholly rejected, for God has provided a believing remnant, even as in the days of Elijah. ' I have left myself seven thousand men, who have not bent the knee to Baal' (Rom. xi, 4; 1 Kings xix, 18). In St. Paul's day a large proportion of the Christians were Jews, including all the apostles; and this war has brought a number of Catholic Jews to our notice, chiefly from Austria. More than this: before the end of the world the Jews as a body will be converted. For it is but a partial hardening that hath befallen Israel, until the full number of the gentiles be entered in, and thus all Israel also shall be saved, according as it is written:

> There shall come from Sion the deliverer,
> he shall banish impieties from Jacob.
> And when I take away their sins,
> this shall be to them my covenant.
>
> (Rom. xi, 25–27: *cf.* Isaiah lix, 20–21.)

It is necessary also in dealing with prophecy to revert to

the principle of compenetration, which I have expounded more than once elsewhere. At the present time it is widely recognized by Catholic exegetes as an important key to a number of Old Testament passages, and none seem to dispute its validity. It is best enunciated in the words of St. Thomas Aquinas in the prooemium to his commentary on the Psalms :

' Prophecies are sometimes uttered about things which existed at the time in question, not primarily with reference to them, but in so far as they are a figure of things to come ; and therefore the Holy Ghost has provided that when such prophecies are uttered, some details should be inserted which go beyond the actual thing done, in order that the mind may be raised to the thing signified.'

He then goes on to explain that in the book of Daniel much is said of Antiochus IV Epiphanes as a figure of Antichrist ; and therefore ' some things are therein read which were not accomplished in the case of Antiochus, but will be fulfilled in Antichrist.' In the same way, he goes on, in Ps. lxxii (Vulg. lxxi : *Deus iudicium*) we read something which exceeds the power of the kingdom of David and Solomon, but shall be fulfilled in the kingdom of Christ, of which that other was a figure.

In all this St. Thomas is obviously following (though without mentioning him) St. Jerome's commentary on Daniel xi, 21 ff., where he enunciates this principle of compenetration as the current Catholic doctrine of his day, and uses the same illustrations. The principle may likewise be seen at work in the ' Passion-Psalm,' Ps. xxii (Vulg. xxi : *Deus, Deus meus*), as is explained, for instance, in the edition of that psalm in the Westminster Version ; and also in Isaiah liii, ' the Passion according to Isaiah,' for the prophet rises to the theme of the Messianic deliverance from that of the deliverance and return from the Babylonian captivity. Other examples might be given.

Not all prophecy, however, takes this form ; for the more direct form it is convenient to refer to the book of

Malachy, in editing which for the Westminster Version I have devoted much attention to the Eucharistic prophecy in Mal. i, 10–11 :

> I take no pleasure in you,
>> saith Jehovah of hosts,
> Neither will I accept an offering
>> at your hand.
> For from the rising of the sun
>> even unto the setting thereof
> My name shall be great among the gentiles,
>> and in every place
> There shall be sacrifice, there shall be offering
>> unto my name, even a pure oblation.

Another prophecy of especial importance is to be found in Gen. xlix, 10, which is best translated :

> The sceptre shall not pass from Judah,
>> nor the staff from between his feet,
> Until he come whose it is,
>> And to him shall be the obedience of the peoples.

The ' sceptre ' is the symbol of civil rule, the ' staff ' of military command. It must be enough to say here that when the last vestige of Jewish autonomy had passed away with the Herods, the Christ had come, to whom belongs all power in heaven and on earth.

A final word must be said about types, which are sometimes called *prophetia realis*, prophecy by fact, the fact being ·a person or thing or event intended by Almighty God to foreshadow some person or thing or event which is to follow it. There can be nothing arbitrary, therefore, in belief in types. They should not be accepted without some basis in revelation ; for a symbol to be accepted as certain, a certain proof is needed from Scripture or tradition. Thus we may naturally infer from John vi, 49–58, that the manna was a type of the Holy Eucharist, and from John xix, 36, that the paschal lamb was a figure of the true Lamb of God (*cf.* John i, 29, 36).

These examples are strongly borne out by Catholic tradition, which suffices of itself to convince us that the patriarch Joseph was a type of Our Lady's husband. Several other reasonably certain examples might be given, all helping to press home the general principle, *Novum Testamentum in Vetere latet, Vetus in Novo patet* : the New Testament lies hid in the Old, the Old lies open in the New.

PART III

THE NEW TESTAMENT

XI

JESUS CHRIST

JESUS CHRIST is the centre of the world's history. If all that precedes leads up to Him, much more is all that follows conditioned by Him. No crabbed investigation into sources can hide that mighty Figure, which for so brief a time is active in Palestine, and soon kindles a fire the whole world over, which even to-day is still growing in force and volume. ' I am the way and the truth and the life ' (John xiv, 6) : in answer to so vast a claim rises a vast *Credo*, never offered so widely, so heartily, so recklessly, one may say, as now, when it is realized how great the cost has been and is and still will be. Jesus Christ is unique, not as a legendary hero, but in an age and place of which much is known : no rival Christ can compete, either as a historical figure in himself, or in his effect upon individuals and upon humanity in the lump. He has set imperishable ideals before mankind which a multitude without number has endeavoured to make its own, while not a few others that have shrunk from embracing them have still admired and praised.

Such be the feeble panegyric here to be offered, not as mere rhetoric or mere sentiment, but as sober reasoning. This general argument has been well put in a recent criticism of *Formgeschichte* and its methods, a subject to which it will be

necessary to return.[1] ' Form critics,' we read—and the
saying is true of many other critics besides—' leave this early
Christian faith and practice suspended in mid-air, without
foundation ; a thing created out of nothing ; a veritable
Melchizedek, without father, without mother, without
genealogy, without beginning of life.[2] And again, ' History
makes it perfectly clear that the emergence of Christianity
on the life of the world was a profoundly significant effect.
Then we can confidently affirm that it had a profoundly
significant cause.' [3]

In much the same strain the late Sir Edwyn Hoskyns and
Mr. Noel Davey, in that remarkable book, *The Riddle of the
New Testament*,[4] had written that :

' any historical reconstruction which leaves an unbridgeable gulf
between the faith of the Primitive Church and the historical
Jesus must be both inadequate and uncritical : inadequate,
because it leaves the origin of the Church unexplained ; and
uncritical, because a critical sifting of the evidence of the New
Testament points towards the Life and Death of Jesus as the
ground of Primitive Christian faith, and points in no other
direction. . . .

' The challenge lies in the history and not in the thought de-
tached from the history, since the history is an integral element
in the new method of thought, and in fact constitutes its surprise
and its scandal. The question, " What manner of man is this ? "
which is so obvious throughout the Synoptic Gospels, is no mere
literary trick of their Editors. It is put, quite as provocatively,
everywhere in the New Testament.'

This is a scholarly verdict upon the documents. No
amount of juggling with supposed sources has succeeded in
making the conclusion plausible that Jesus was a nobody, who
did nothing in particular : that after spending two or three
years in uttering some beautiful morality and some mistaken

---

[1] *Studies in History and Religion*, presented to Dr. H. Wheeler Robinson,
M.A., ed. Ernest A. Payne, B.A., B.D., B.Litt. Lutterworth Press, 1942.
No. V : ' *Formgeschichte* ' *and its Limitations*, by L. H. Marshall, B.A., B.D.
[2] *Op. cit.*, p. 84.
[3] *Ibid.*, p. 85.
[4] Faber and Faber, 1931 : pp. 246–7, 262–3.

prophecy, He was executed on account of some points in His teaching that seemed to favour revolt from Rome. Such a conclusion does not explain the tremendous upheaval accomplished in that short time, the bitter opposition of His enemies and the fervent devotion of His followers : nor yet the still greater upheaval in the world's history, the rapid development of a movement which soon became the most important factor in the world's history and has remained so ever since, in spite of all the learning and cunning and brutal violence turned against it.

Nor is it possible on the literary plane to work back plausibly to a source which will thus reduce the Saviour's Person and work. Critical, no less than historical, analysis still leaves us confronted with the crucial question, already quoted from Hoskyns and Davey, ' What manner of man is this ? ' Upon the question of sources more will be said in the sequel ; for the present it must be enough to have insisted upon the convergence of all the evidence to produce a single solution, and to consider what that solution is. Not ours (thank God) to emulate the perplexities of the unfortunate man in William de Morgan's *Joseph Vance*,[1] who ' always seemed to me to be endeavouring to find a sieve that would let Christ through and keep the Miracles out.' The very fact of the unity and consistency of the evidence is no small proof that it is reliable.

There is a mingling of terrible weakness and terrible strength. Christ endures to be heckled and calumniated, and goes from failure to failure. Only once is there some appearance of His employing force, and then He was directly concerned, not with His own position, but with His Father's glory. No doubt His righteous anger was compelling ; but, on the other hand, there can be little doubt that His zeal for the holiness of the Temple, which was being made into a den of thieves, would find much popular support. Apart from that, He yields to hostility, and after He has tried Judah, Galilee and Transjordan in turn, nothing further remains but to return to Jerusalem to face a horrible death. His enemies

---

[1] Nelson : p. 455.

had pursued Him relentlessly with words, doing all they could to disturb His ministry, and not without success ; they did not fail to proceed to deeds, when once they saw their chance, and to ensure that He was put to death with all imaginable barbarity. This was the very climax of weakness, to be led as a sheep to the slaughter, to be reduced to the semblance of a worm and no man.

Nevertheless, Christ manifested a power divine. Even His speech was the language of authority, fearless in the face of enmity and attack, even while endowed with a winning charm which has never faded through the centuries. It was no small claim that He put forward ; rather there was no limit to His claim, so that (to speak humanly) only a strong man could have maintained it. Of his miracles something has already been said ; it is impossible to eliminate them from the story, and least of all the Resurrection, prophesied at least three times according to the common source of the synoptic gospels, and early confirmed by the ample evidence known to St. Paul (1 Cor. xv). The apostles, indeed, looked upon it as their special task to bear witness to the Resurrection (Acts i, 22 : ii, 32 : 1 Cor. ix, 1 : *etc.*).

The answer to this great antinomy is love. ' For God so loved the world, that He gave His only begotten Son, that whosoever believeth in Him may not perish, but may have everlasting life ' (John iii, 16). If we are prepared to allow for the high purposes of Almighty God, instead of (with some perverse students) seeking to explain everything away by the most degraded practices of the savage, we shall see some foreshadowing of the Redemption in the sacrifice of Isaac. Christ Himself claimed to be the Good Shepherd, who would lay down His life for His sheep, in obedience to His Father's command, but likewise out of love for man which He shared with His Father : ' Greater love than this no man hath, than that he lay down his life for his friends ' (John x, 11, 18 : xv, 13). He came ' not to be served but to serve, and to give His life a ransom for many ' (Matt. xx, 28 : Mark x, 45). The Cross was not merely the altar of His sacrifice, but the chair of His teaching ; man was to learn to covet riches and glory and pleasure no more, but to climb the now royal road of Calvary.

Already in the early heresies and apocryphal gospels we see the revulsion from this. According to some of these there was left upon the Cross a mere dummy, from which the Divine Person had withdrawn. The story of the Infancy was also ' written up ' in such a way as to brush away (if so it could be) the shadow of the Cross, and to leave only majesty and power. But the canonical gospels tell another story. The angels line the heavens to proclaim Messiah's birth, but Simeon foretells that a sword shall pierce His mother's heart ; the Magi come from the east with their offerings to do him homage, but He has to be rushed off to Egypt to escape being murdered.

The late Dr. Montague James, indeed, in the preface to his valuable book, *The Apocryphal New Testament*,[1] has borne competent witness to the contrast between the canonical and the apocryphal literature. The authors of the latter, he says,

' do not speak with the voices of Paul or of John, or with the quiet simplicity of the three first Gospels. It is not unfair to say that when they attempt the former tone, they are theatrical, and when they essay the latter, they are jejune. In short, the result of anything like an attentive study of the literature, in bulk and in detail, is an added respect for the sense of the Church Catholic, and for the wisdom of the scholars of Alexandria, Antioch, and Rome : assuredly in this case they were tried money-changers, who proved all things and held fast that which was good.'

Dr. James writes a little too much as if it were only literary taste and scholarship that taught the Catholic Church her canon, rather than her own divine tradition ; but still, his judgment upon the literary and historical issue is a reliable one, and should have weight even with those who do not respect the Catholic tradition.

For those who have understood this divine plan in the life of Christ, it will be easy to recognize the same traits in the

[1] Oxford, at the Clarendon Press, 1924 : p. XII.

life of the Church, ' which is His body, the fulness of Him who is wholly fulfilled in all ' (Ephes. i, 23). There is the same weakness : the Church has been persecuted by those without: and even those who claimed to be her children have usurped powers which were rightly hers. Politicians, authors, scholars, all have pointed the finger of scorn at her, displaying for the most part a colossal ignorance of her real character, and bringing enormous evils on the world by denying her claims to teach Christian faith and morals, and hindering her sacred mission. ' The natural man doth not accept the teaching of the Spirit of God, for to him it is folly, and he cannot understand it ' (1 Cor. ii, 14). And there is worse than all this : ' it must needs be that scandals come ' (Matt. xviii, 7 : cf. Luke xvii, 1). The Church is the Church not merely of John and Peter, the innocent and the penitent, but also of Judas.

Nevertheless, to those who have eyes to see, she manifests divine power. Upon this subject the Vatican Council speaks with no uncertain voice :

' Nay, the Church in herself, by reason of her marvellous expansion, her unique holiness, and inexhaustible richness in all good things, of her Catholic unity and invincible stability, is a great and perpetual motive of belief, and an irrefutable witness to her own divine mission.' [1]

While she is ever increasing in sheer numbers, she is likewise for ever clarifying her doctrine and growing in holiness and zeal, ever penetrating better the mind of her Lord even in her ideals of conduct. The gross heresies and the gross scandals of other days appear now (thank God) to be almost impossible, and the choice lies between her and a lapse into appalling chaos. And Christ loves the Church (Ephes. v, 25) ; often as her death and decay are announced, it is not she that perishes, but her persecutors.

Here, too, the key to the mystery is love : not the mere unaided love of man, but the charity of God Himself, which is poured forth into the hearts of the faithful (Rom. v, 5), so

[1] Sess. III, ch. 3.

that they not only respond with love and devotion and sacrifice, but include in that love and devotion and sacrifice both those within the fold and those without. No doubt there is always much room for progress, and always will be; nevertheless, the accomplishment is unique, in all that is done and endured for the poor and the sick and the children both at home and in the foreign missions, and in much else besides.

It is this large view of Jesus Christ that we must take if we would wish (however imperfectly) to understand Him : the Christ of the whole New Testament, the Christ of the Church Catholic in all times and places : the Christ who not only speaks to us from without through Church and sacrament and sacrifice and in all that are His, but who also works upon us from within through His Holy Spirit, so that we no longer live our own life, but it is Christ (so far as we suffer Him) that lives within us, and all that would resist Him is crucified (Galat. ii, 19–20). Such an understanding the Apostle prayed for his Christians :

> ' that he grant you according to the riches of his glory to be strengthened powerfully through his Spirit in the inward man—that Christ may dwell in your hearts through faith, so that, rooted and founded in charity, ye may be able to comprehend with all the saints what is the breadth and length and height and depth—yea, to know the charity of Christ which surpasseth knowledge, that ye may be filled unto all the fulness of God '. (Ephes. iii, 16–19).

To such an understanding the greatest difficulty nowadays appears to be the opinion that Christ expected to return in glory for the last judgment immediately after His execution, the mention of which precedes the texts upon which this view most relies. Some of those standing by are not to taste death until they see ' the Son of man coming in his kingdom ' (Matt. xvi, 28), ' the kingdom of God coming in power ' (Mark ix, 1), or in Luke simply ' until they see the kingdom of God ' (Luke ix, 27). We notice at once a certain vagueness in these expressions. Although Our Lord has just said that He is to come with His angels, He does not make it clear that it is precisely this event to which He is referring. Nor is it likely that He was so understood; for even the Resurrection would not have sufficed for His apostles and disciples if they had thought that He had made a false prophecy of the last judgment, nor (to put it on the lowest ground) can we imagine the evangelists recording such a refutation both of His mission and their own preaching.

The best explanation appears to be that Christ was referring to the destruction of Jerusalem. There was a judgment of universal import, wherein each should receive according to his works (Matt. xvi, 27), hanging over the whole world; but some even of those standing by were to see, as it were, its chief rehearsal, the final closing of the Old Covenant by a tremendous act of the God-man's power. Having now founded His Church securely among the gentiles, He would cast out the original children of the kingdom, for whom it was primarily intended, from Temple and covenant, and have their city destroyed. We cannot easily magnify the significance in the divine plan of the destruction of Jerusalem, to be consummated in a second destruction not so long after. The first destruction fits the expression, 'some of those standing by,' for a number of them would have died. And this same interpretation is supported by the fairly obvious meaning of the other passage which is brought up in this connection. It is found in practically the same form in all three synoptic gospels: 'This generation shall not pass away until all these things come to pass' (Matt. xxiv, 34, etc.).

Christ had certainly been speaking of the destruction of Jerusalem; and He had certainly passed on from that to speak of the destruction of the world. It is true that in Matt. xxiv, 29, we read 'immediately after the tribulations of those days'; but 'immediately,' as we can see from its frequent use in Mark, is really a vaguer word than it sounds, a fact probably to be explained by the usage in Aramaic of its equivalent. In Mark xiii, 24, the words 'in those days, after that tribulation,' do not necessarily give any indication of time. In Luke xxi, 25, we simply read 'and.'

After these paragraphs on the end of the world comes the parable of the fig tree, which offers definite signs of an end already known to be near, which the generation then living is to see, which is plainly the destruction of Jerusalem : then we read, ' but about *that* day and hour,' the date of the end of the world, ' none knoweth, not the angels in heaven nor the Son.' It may be noticed in passing that the common Catholic doctrine is that Christ knew the day even in His human nature, but that it did not fall within the scope of His mission to communicate it. But when He has laid so much stress on the general ignorance of the day, it is surely perverse exegesis to refer it to a day which He has said to be coming within the lifetime of some of His hearers, with definite signs to herald it.

There is sufficient indication even in the context that such a distinction should be made ; and it is strengthened by other passages in the gospels. Many are to come from east and west and to recline with Abraham and Isaac and Jacob in the kingdom of heaven (*cf.* Matt. viii, 11 : Luke xiii, 29 : *cf.* Mal. i, 11) ; this supposes a considerable work of evangelization, not to be supposed complete in a lifetime. The conclusion is pressed home by other passages. The kingdom is to be taken away from the Jews, and given to a nation that will yield the fruits thereof (Matt. xxi, 43) ; insistence upon this is characteristic of the first gospel (*cf.* p. 99). Even in the introduction to the discourse on the end of Jerusalem and the world, it is said that the gospel of the kingdom must be preached in the whole world for a testimony to all the nations before the end comes (Matt. xxiv, 14 : *cf.* Mark xiii, 10), a task hardly achieved even yet. It was upon this task that Our Lord laid stress before ascending to the Father. He bade His apostles make disciples of all the nations, and promised to be with them Himself to the end of time (Matt. xxviii, 19–20), a commission repeated in the long ending to Mark (Mark xvi, 15). St. Luke also testifies to it, both in his gospel (xxiv, 47) and in the Acts (i, 8).

Much other witness might be quoted to the same effect, but one more passage will be enough. A simple maiden visiting her ancient kinswoman in the hill-country of Judah bursts into a canticle of praise, redolent of the Old Testament, like all else in those first two chapters of Luke. Few are present, and they are but little known to their countrymen ; nevertheless, in spite of this, and in spite of the profound humility of her thanksgiving, the Holy Spirit moves her to speak momentous words : ' Henceforth all generations shall call me blessed.' A marvellous prophecy, amply fulfilled in the Catholic Church ; but for our present purpose it must suffice to point out that evidently she did not contemplate merely one or two generations, but looked well beyond them.

XII

MARK

I⊤ is plain even to the more casual reader that the first three gospels bear a close relation to each other, while the fourth gospel stands somewhat apart. This last, accordingly, will be considered later on, and for the present we must be content to confine our attention to Matthew, Mark and Luke. These three are called the 'synoptic' gospels : this term, we read in the great *Oxford English Dictionary*, 'is applied distinctively to the first three Gospels as giving an account of the events from the same point of view or under the same general aspect.' This is the explanation most likely to appeal to students of the 'synoptic problem,' the problem of the mutual relations of these gospels ; but another current explanation is found, for example, in the *Concise Oxford Dictionary*, that the term is applied to them as 'affording a conspectus or general survey,' presumably of Christ's life and teaching. This seems the less happy explanation.

In the first place there is a considerable amount of narrative common to the synoptic gospels, covering the public ministry of Our Lord, the Passion, and (to judge from the gospel parallels) at least the discovery of the empty tomb, the vision of the angels, and the return of the holy women. This common narrative embraces many utterances of Our Lord, usually forming part of historical incidents, but occasionally there are set discourses in the shape of parables, and there is also the unique 'little apocalypse,' a prophecy of the end of Jerusalem and of the world (Matt. xxiv, *etc.*). This common matter may be said to form the substance of the gospels. But Matthew also contains several set discourses

[89]

or continuous speeches of Our Lord; these to a large extent appear also in Luke, where, however, they are more scattered, in a way that suggests more deliberate arrangement in Matthew, governed at times by logical rather than chronological considerations. Finally, each evangelist contributes matter of his own, not merely in the way of separate incidents or sayings, but also in his handling of what is already common synoptic matter. In this editorial work each evangelist displays strong characteristics of his own.

This must suffice as a very rough outline of the contents of the synoptic gospels; the synoptic problem contains many intricacies which do not fall within the scope of the present work. To deal now first with the gospel of St. Mark, it may be laid down with some confidence that it did not serve as a source to Matthew and Luke. This statement runs counter to the widely held opinion that Matthew and Luke are composed of Mark *plus* the *Logia* or *Q* (about which in the next chapter) and later editorial matter. Such a view is so inconsistent with the linguistic evidence that it seems unlikely to prevail for long. Mark, in fact, reacts against the common source in the same way as Matthew and Luke, though to a lesser extent than they.

This is a fact which can easily be verified in the late Sir John Hawkins' *Horae Synopticae*,[1] in which the main statistics are presented with admirable relevance and lucidity. There is a certain bias in the work in favour of the ' Two-document hypothesis,' but this only makes the weight of evidence adduced on the other side all the more telling. In the tables on pp. 12–13 the occurrences of words and phrases characteristic of Mark, as compared with the other gospels and the rest of the New Testament, reach the formidable total of 357. It is to be remembered, too, that the characteristic words and phrases ' are rather more thickly scattered over the small peculiar portions than they are over the large common portions ' (p. 26) : that is to say, the more the writer is free

---

[1] *Horae Synopticae : Contributions to the Study of the Synoptic Problem.* By the Rev. Sir John C. Hawkins, Bart., M.A., D.D.; ed. 2. Oxford, at the Clarendon Press, 1909.

from the restraining influence of the common source, the more he exhibits his own peculiar style. This is true also of the other synoptists, but (once more) to a lesser extent of Mark.

Having, however, adopted the view that the use of Mark as a basis or *Grundschrift* ' may now (1909) be called a practically certain result of modern study of the synoptic problem ' (p. 115), Sir John proceeds to devote pp. 114-153 to the not very easy task of explaining how Matthew and Luke, together or singly, omit or alter what they found in their supposed *Grundschrift* ; but at the end he still holds fast to his belief that they used Mark ' almost as we have it now. Almost ; but not quite ' (p. 152). It is not worth while to linger upon the few small points which he then raises, but we may pass at once to pp. 208-212, where he considers ' the alterations and small additions in which Matthew and Luke agree against Mark.' Of these he has found in all about 218 (p. 209 : 100 and 118) ; ' only approximate numbers are given,' he writes, ' because of variant readings,' but once again the figure is no small one. In regard to some his view is that ' it seems almost impossible that Matthew and Luke could have accidentally concurred in making them. In these cases at least the changes seem to be owing to some influence, direct or indirect, of a common source, and not to the independent judgment of two compilers.'

In his first edition Sir John was of opinion that such agreements of Matthew and Luke against Mark arose ' in the course of that oral transmission which, as we have seen (pp. 67, 78), is almost required by other phenomena of the Gospels.' But in his second edition it appears to him that ' perhaps the majority ' of them may be best accounted for by Dr. Sanday's suggestion that Matthew and Luke used ' a recension of the text of Mark different from that from which all the extant MSS. of the Gospel are derived ' (p. 212). Thus we come back after all to the rather desperate expedient of an *Ur-Marcus*, a primitive Mark, which has left no trace behind it, but which is urgently required to keep out any element of oral transmission. Sir John was the very full and reliable statistician of the synoptic seminar which met at Oxford under Dr. Sanday's presidency, and which later published its *Studies in the Synoptic Problem* (Oxford, 1911) under Dr. Sanday's editorship, and in that book Dr. Sanday was to lead off with a paper upon ' the conditions under which the gospels were written '; it is no great wonder if Sir John abandoned his defence of oral transmission in the face of a strong and united team battling under such leadership. I gratefully acknowledge the profit derived in these studies from the seminar in general and from Dr. Sanday in particular, but when he writes in his paper that ' the Evangelists thought of themselves not merely as copyists but as historians ' (p. 12), I should think it safe to say that they thought of themselves as neither ; they had a higher and more urgent task before them, that of supplying essential instruction to the first Christians in an accessible form.

That Mark comes nearest to the common source is obvious, and can easily be shown from *Horae Synopticae*; it is indeed the evidence making for this conclusion which has led so many to suppose it to be the common source itself, to the neglect of the many signs of editorial work. They have also overlooked the strong indications of the working of memory in the composition of the synoptic gospels. In the first place, a minute inspection shows that the similarity between the gospels is not so close as we might expect from the mere copying of documents ; thus, if we take the Westcott-Hort text as our standard, there are under twenty verses of any of the three gospels which are found as they stand in any of the others, and even of these two are Old Testament quotations. In the second place, the nature of the likenesses and differences must be taken into account ; where a verse is most easily remembered (as for example when it consists of some striking saying) the parallel passages resemble each other closest, and *vice versa*. Thirdly, the changes in order between the gospels do not always find a plausible explanation other than that which might at times obtain in our own case ; they did not remember the historical sequence of the incidents—and indeed sometimes had little or nothing to help them to do so—and did not mean to commit themselves to it. Sometimes, on the contrary, we find the association of ideas at work; one saying leads to another of like import, and thus we gain a fuller grasp of Our Lord's meaning from the play of the evangelist's memory. The best parallel phenomenon is to be found in the liturgies, where a fixed form of words, corresponding to the common source, came to be varied a certain amount in different times and places, partly because it was largely recited from memory, partly because changes were deliberately instituted or admitted which were thought to be improvements. There is no need to deny that written documents may have played some part in the transmission both of the narrative and discourse matter; but the above considerations tend to show that the chief factors at work were oral tradition and memory.

It seems more likely that the narrative source existed almost from the beginning as one whole, though there is less reason to suppose this of the discourse matter common to Matthew and Luke, but absent from Mark. If we try to take a concrete and realistic view of the first preaching of the gospel, we shall understand that some account of Christ's life and death, short and easily remembered, must have been needed practically at once. Into this account His discourses would gradually come to be inserted. But the presentation of them in Matthew bears too many signs of deliberate arrangement and rhetorical art to be quite primitive; and the impression thus derived from this gospel is confirmed by the fact that sayings which are grouped together logically in Matthew are found scattered in different parts of Luke.

To say that there was a common narrative source is not of course to deny that it is composed of units of different kinds, or that the several kinds each deserve careful consideration, such as the modern *Formgeschichte* ('Form-history') devotes to them. The complaint against this new method is rather that in its estimate of the evidence it is unwarrantably sceptical. Such a complaint finds adequate expression in the contribution (already mentioned in chap. XI) to *Studies in History and Religion*, by Mr. Marshall. He insists (p. 76) on the quite natural character of the forms actually found: parables, miracle-stories and the rest: there is no reasonable

BACK TO THE BIBLE

ground for suspecting them. ' The new critical method,' he writes, ' has severe limitations. Its chief defect is that it allows subjectivity and arbitrariness such free play that they are apt positively to run riot' (p. 77). And again, after quoting a glaring example of this : ' Such reconstructions of the history of the Synoptic tradition can safely be brushed aside as utterly worthless, for a critical method of this kind—like the allegorical interpretation of Scripture— is comparable to a witch's broomstick on which one can travel whithersoever one wishes to go ' (p. 80).

The stress laid on Mark as itself the narrative source is odd, not merely from the linguistic and statistical point of view, but also by reason of the contents. It is put forward as (more or less) the one reliable gospel ; yet it is preeminently the gospel of miracle, and miracles the modern critic will not have. It is an ugly and (at first acquaintance) a startling fact that miracles are tacitly assumed not to have happened ; this, as has been remarked at the beginning of chap. II, is no longer a question of evidence, but of presuppositions. St. Mark's main interest is not in the discourses, but in the miracles. According to a strong and early tradition he based his gospel on the teaching of St. Peter ; and he may be said to take for the theme of his gentile gospel St. Peter's first great utterance to the gentiles in regard of Christ: ' He is Lord of all ' (Acts x, 36). In this gospel it is not by words so much as by deeds that Christ proclaims His divine mission ; it is not so very surprising if some of those who look upon Mark as the best source for Christ's life, and nevertheless reject the deeds, have come to look upon the whole gospel story as a myth. And yet history, too, has her legitimate claims ; and if the presuppositions of some critics lead them to reject such a mass of evidence, the verdict of history must surely be, so much the worse for the presuppositions. We are dealing here immediately with Mark, which may be said to supply the acid test ; but it has already been pointed out in the last chapter, à propos of *The Riddle of the New Testament* (p. 93) that the same is true of the New Testament as a whole.

[94]

XIII

MATTHEW

In itself it is not a point of major moment who wrote the
gospels, provided that they are shown to be reliable ; but
this very proof depends to a varying extent upon the authorship.   In the case of the third and fourth gospels the question
of authorship is of great importance, because we know much
about the authors ; it is of less importance in the case of the
first and second gospels.   It can hardly be regarded as quite
certain that the author of the gospel is the John Mark of the
Acts, or the founder of the Alexandrian Church ; on the
other hand, it seems fairly safe to accept him as the Mark of
the epistles, the cousin of Barnabas, the ' son ' of Peter
(Col. iv, 10 : 2 Tim. iv, 11 : Philem. 24 : 1 Pet. v, 13).   Of
Matthew we know even less.   The fact that in the first
gospel it is made clear (Matt. ix, 9) that it is the apostle who
was the publican certainly helps the identification of the
author and apostle ; but we should need much more internal
evidence of the same kind to make up a really weighty argument.   The internal evidence, soon to be summarized, is of
great importance, but as a guarantee of the trustworthiness
of the author, which does not go far to indicate who precisely
he was.

On the other hand, the external evidence is very strong, not
merely indicating a reliable author in general, but naming
him as the apostle Matthew.   Indeed, the external evidence
for all the four gospels is strong.   Before the end of the
second century the gospels can be shown to be in use in the
leading churches under the names of the authors.   When we
have the voluminous writers, who cover a considerable

amount of ground in their works, such as Irenaeus in Gaul, Clement and Origen at Alexandria, and Tertullian in Africa, we find the evangelists known by name; and early in the fourth century Eusebius, whom we may call the first serious student of the history of the canon, knows of no serious dispute about the matter. St. Justin Martyr may be regarded as an exception in not naming them, but he knows of the apostles' 'memoirs,' called 'gospels' (1 Apol. cc. 66–77: Dial. c. 103), and quotes all four of them. Perhaps he thought that it would detract from his philosophic style and weight if he named their Jewish authors; in any case we can be sure of the Roman tradition from St. Irenaeus and the Muratorian fragment.

The earlier writers deal with special themes and occasions, and more shortly; we cannot expect them to enumerate the New Testament writers, but they quote the works themselves, and were evidently handing on traditions about their authorship, as about so much else. The total evidence for the authorship of the four gospels is thus overwhelming, as it is likewise for the integrity of the text. It is a pity that those who assault the genuineness and the text of the gospels and other New Testament writings do not seem as a rule to have had much experience of similar studies in the neutral field of classical authors, where their methods would be regarded as intolerable cynicism. We do not regard Sophocles as a myth because his text depends in the main upon the famous Laurentian manuscript of the eleventh century, nor yet Catullus, the evidence for whose works is later still; and so of other classical authors, none of whom can be compared with the New Testament writers, and least of all the evangelists, in regard of external and textual attestation.

In the case of Matthew and Mark, we have one unusually early testimony to the authorship preserved by Eusebius in an important chapter of his *Church History* (Bk. III, chap. 39). The enquiries which Papias tells us that he made probably belong to the first century. Eusebius quotes him as writing that ' Matthew wrote the oracles in the Hebrew dialect, and each translated them as best he could.' In the first place it should be noticed that by ' Hebrew ' must be understood what would nowadays be called Aramaic, the native language of the Jews in New Testament times, picked up from their neighbours after the exile. The word is used with this meaning in the New Testament and early writers ; Aramaic, in fact, is so like Hebrew as scarcely to deserve to be called a separate language, and besides, a number of the writers did not know either of the languages, and so were the less likely to distinguish between them. It is far more likely that St. Matthew would write in Aramaic than in Hebrew, and in some cases external evidence is clear upon the point. St. Matthew, according to Papias, wrote the *Logia,* a Greek word here translated ' oracles,' a word used to signify the divine inspiration of Holy Writ. St. Paul applies the word to the Old Testament in Rom. iii, 2, as the learned Jewish philosopher Philo was doing about the same time. It came early to be applied also to the New Testament, the first so to use it being apparently St. Polycarp, the disciple of St. John, in his epistle to the Philippians (chap. 7). Grenfell and Hunt no doubt found ' The Logia of Jesus ' an arresting title for their finds of Christ's supposed sayings ; but the word ' Logia ' does not appear to have been used in the papyri themselves, and it is significant that Moulton and Milligan in their *Vocabulary of the New Testament illustrated from the Papyri,* write (s.v.) that they are unable to throw any fresh light upon the word. Indeed, the letter Q has now commonly replaced it as the symbol of the discourse document supposed to be a common element in Matthew and Luke.

Papias, as quoted in the same chapter of Eusebius, reports that ' the Presbyter '—apparently meaning St. John the Apostle—used to say that St. Mark wrote down accurately what he remembered of St. Peter's teaching ; and St. Peter, he implies, was not writing a gospel, but was engaged in practical instruction. But we gather that even if Peter had intended to produce a gospel such as Mark's, it would still have been a book of oracles about the Lord ; the contents would still have been ' Logia,' not as being sayings, but as being inspired. Finally, it should be remembered in regard

of Matthew that Eusebius also makes it clear that both he
himself and St. Irenaeus knew Papias' *Expositions of the
Oracles about the Lord*, a work no longer extant, and it is
inconceivable that neither of them should have given any
hint that Papias understood St. Matthew's work to be merely
a collection of Christ's sayings. It seems likely that Papias
was commenting on the whole New Testament.

Papias' statement that St. Matthew wrote in Hebrew (*i.e.*,
in Aramaic) is confirmed by other ancient authorities, and
especially by Jerome, who sees in the so-called ' Gospel
according to the Hebrews ' the *ipsum hebraicum*, the original
Hebrew text of the gospel ; and this witness cannot lightly
be set aside, for he also remarks that he has lately translated
it into Greek and Latin (*De Viris Illustribus*, cc. 2–3). The
early references to this ' gospel ' and the quotations from it
have been edited by Preuschen in his *Antilegomena* (Giessen,
1901), and translated by Dr. James in his *Apocryphal New
Testament* (Oxford, 1924). The quotations are surprisingly
different from our Matthew, of which it was doubtless a
mutilated version ; St. Jerome would naturally choose
passages of this kind for quotation, and not those which
agreed with the canonical Matthew. The very fact that he
thought it worth while to translate the work shows that he
was aware that it contained notable variations from the
canonical text ; and this explains why he hesitates in some
passages to call it outright the original Matthew. Although
he speaks of it sometimes as written in Hebrew, he makes it
clear in one passage that he means Aramaic, saying that it is
written *Chaldaico Syroque sermone* ; [1] and in another he cites
a couple of Aramaic words as St. Matthew's own.[2] That the
Aramaic text of Matthew has perished is not surprising,
seeing how little demand there would soon be for it ; Josephus
tells us at the beginning of his *Jewish War* that it was written
originally in Aramaic, but in this case, too, the original Aramaic
was doubtless lost for lack of readers.

That the gospel is intensely Jewish has been sufficiently
shown in the introduction devoted to it in the Westminster

[1] *Contra Pelag.* III, 2 : Preuschen, p. 4.   [2] *Ep. 5 ad Damas* : Preuschen, p. 6.

Version ; it is, in fact, the only thoroughly Jewish gospel, and in this way contrasts with the others, which are as plainly written for gentiles. The Jewish traits are summed up under the four headings of information, outlook, use of the Old Testament, and style. It is a strongly controversial work, being written not merely for Christian but also for non-Christian Jews. Against these latter it presses home arguments from the Old Testament, and it insists again and again on God's rejection of the Jews and call of the gentiles. Whereas St. Mark thinks it necessary to explain to gentile readers the Jews' frequent washing of hands and cups and the like (vii, 3–4), St. Matthew does not stop to explain how the Temple service took precedence over sabbath obligations (xii, 5), though gentile readers were not likely to understand the point.

This very character of the gospel lets us see that it must have been written at an early date, where and when the Jewish issue was a very living one for the early Church. It was the failure to allow sufficiently for this that led the late Dr. Streeter in his work, *The Four Gospels* (Macmillan, 1924), which otherwise contains much of value, to adopt the strange hypothesis (taken up also by Dr. Cadoux [1]) that the gospel was produced at Antioch about A.D. 85 (p. 150), that is to say, in a great gentile church, after the evangelization of the Jews had lost so much of its hope and force. If the supposition of a Greek Matthew requires such an origin as this, it stands self-condemned ; possibly, however, the admission of an Aramaic Matthew might open a way to reconciliation, because the standard Greek translation would doubtless be made later under the influence of the other synoptic gospels.

Another point which has often been missed is the extremely Matthaean character of the first two chapters. Left to himself, without the restraint imposed upon him by his sources, the evangelist gives freer play to his own linguistic tendencies. Sir John Hawkins remarks (*Horae Synopticae*, p. 9) that his characteristic words and phrases ' are used

[1] *The Historic Mission of Jesus*, p. 22. Lutterworth Press, 1941.

BACK TO THE BIBLE

considerably more freely in these two chapters than in the rest of the book.' This is in keeping with his general conclusion that the characteristic words and phrases ' are very much more abundant in the peculiar (*i.e.*, unparalleled) than in the common portions of the Gospel ' (*ibid.*, p. 10). The genealogy is obviously a Jewish feature, and remains so even in ' Mary's gospel ' in Luke, which is also strongly Jewish ; but it is further characteristic of Matthew to make especial mention of three gentile women in Christ's ancestry, and even of Uriah, who was not His ancestor. This is in keeping with his general emphasis on the call of the gentiles and the rejection of the Jews, also implied in the coming of the Magi, to whom high priests and scribes point the way, but do not take it. The use of the Old Testament, too, is very free, after the rabbinical fashion, even to seeing a fulfilment of prophecy in Christ being a Nazarene, and that without explaining how. The Messiah was to be the Branch, *nezer* (Isai. xi, 1), and St. Matthew sees at least a partial fulfilment of this title in His coming from Nazareth—from ' Branchtown,' as we might say. Even the dream-guidance is repeated for Pilate's wife (Matt. xxvii, 19).

Upon the historical side the convergence of Luke from a totally different standpoint makes the Virgin Birth one of the most strongly attested facts in the gospels ; in Matthew the story is evidently told from the point of view of St. Joseph, as in Luke from that of the Blessed Virgin herself. By way of external confirmation we may notice that the apocryphal *Assumption of Moses*, probably written a little before the opening of the public ministry, writes (as a pretended prophecy) of Herod the Great that ' he will slay the old and the young, and he will not spare ' (chap. VI, sect. 4) ; the special mention of ' the young ' may be a reference to the murder of the Holy Innocents. The references to the Virgin Birth in Jewish attacks and apocryphal gospels likewise go back to an early date.[1]

[1] *Cf. Christianity in Talmud and Midrash*, by R. Travers Herford (Williams & Norgate, 1903), e.g., pp. 357–8 ; Justin's *Dialogue with Trypho*, ch. lxvii ; and the *Protevangel of James*, assigned by Dr. Montague James to the second century (*The Apocryphal New Testament*, p. 38).

MATTHEW

St. John's gospel is considered in chap. XVI. For those who regard the doctrine therein contained as nothing but later theology, some of the characteristic passages of Matthew will come under the same condemnation ; but in reality each gospel justifies the other, and both (as has been pointed out in chap. XI) are supported by the New Testament as a whole. It is only in Matthew, for instance, that Christ speaks of His despatching His angels (xiii, 41) or His prophets (xxiii, 34 : cf. Luke xi, 49) ; but what appears to be the most significant passage of all, with reference to the mutual knowledge of Father and Son, is also found in Luke (Matt. xi, 27 : Luke x, 22). Nor are such sayings limited to the discourse-matter common to Matthew and Luke ; they are found also in the narrative common to all three synoptic gospels. Early in the ministry a leper says to Christ, ' Lord, if thou wilt, thou canst make me clean ' ; and He answers, ' I will : be thou made clean.' In the next episode the scribes and pharisees think that He is blaspheming because He has told the paralytic that his sins are forgiven : ' Who can forgive sins save God alone ? ' But Christ takes up the challenge : ' that ye may know that the Son of Man hath power on earth to forgive sins '—and then He works the miracle (Mark i, 40–ii, 12 : Luke v, 12–26 : Matt. viii, 1–4 : ix, 2–8). A human confessor would hasten to say that he had no such power of his own, and was only acting in virtue of a divine commission ; but Christ holds quite other language, and works a miracle to confirm it. And this is Mark, with Matthew and Luke running parallel !

XIV

LUKE

St. Luke's two volumes must here be taken together. In dealing with the gospel of St. John it is not worth while to bring the Apocalypse into the discussion, because in the present state of non-Catholic opinion it is likely to raise more difficulties than it solves ; in the present work a few remarks are made about it merely for its own sake. With the Acts of the Apostles it is otherwise ; it is plain that the book was written by the same author as the gospel, and it is even plainer from the Acts than from the gospel that the author was a reliable historian. The two books may almost be reckoned two volumes of a single work, as indeed is suggested by their common dedication to Theophilus ; and the story of the Ascension is the link which binds them together, the shorter account in the gospel looking back to the life of Christ, and the longer account in the Acts looking forward to the life of the Church.

The *external* evidence to the Lucan authorship of gospel and Acts is strong ; it may be enough here to indicate some from St. Irenaeus, writing in the second half of the second century. He was in touch with the churches of Asia Minor, where in his early life he had known St. Polycarp, the disciple of St. John ; and also with the church of Rome, to which he was sent as a priest with high commendation from his own persecuted church of Lyons, whereof he afterwards became bishop. He has been mentioned already as a witness to the genuineness of the four gospels early in chap. XIII ; he mentions all four evangelists, for example, in his great work *Against Heresies*, in Bk. III, chap. I, no. 1, and again in

LUKE

chap. XI, no. 7. In cc. XII–XIV he quotes freely from the Acts as written by St. Luke, who was ' inseparable from Paul ' (chap. XIV, no. 1) : he quotes Acts iv, 22, with the formula, ' the Scripture saith ' : he calls the work itself ' the Acts of the Apostles ' (chap. XIII, no. 3). Other testimony abounds.

A consideration of the chief *internal* evidence that the *same* author wrote gospel and Acts (abstracting meanwhile from the question whether this same author was Luke) will help us to realize some of that author's characteristics. The identity of authorship is indeed asserted in the very first words of the Acts, which obviously refer to the third gospel, itself dedicated in its opening sentence to Theophilus. At the first impression the style of the writing does not favour such identity. There are at least six styles in the Lucan writings : the pronounced Old Testament style of the first two chapters of the gospel : the rather less pronounced Old Testament style of the early part of the Acts : the most natural style, the easy flowing narrative of St. Paul's ministry, which is the main theme of the Acts (though there are passages here and there which do not run so smoothly) : the rather more cramped Lucan style in the gospel, when it is incorporating common sources and loses something of its own freedom in the process : the intermediate Lucan style of the independent gospel passages : and the elaborate sentence which opens the gospel, a quite unique literary effort on the part of its author.

Nevertheless, all this diversity has not hindered Sir John Hawkins, for instance, from writing that ' on the whole there is an immense balance of internal and linguistic evidence in favour of the view that the original writer of these sections was the same person as the main author of the Acts and of the third Gospel, and, consequently, that the date of those books lies within the lifetime of a companion of St. Paul ' (*Horae Synopticae*, ed. 2, pp. 188–9). The sections referred to are the so-called ' we-sections,' to be explained shortly. It is of course impossible here to reproduce the carefully compiled tables upon which Sir John's conclusions are based. From these, however, one fact stands out clearly, that it is precisely a characteristic of St. Luke to have a *plastic* style, which he consciously or unconsciously adapts to the subject-matter with which he is dealing ; and this again fits in well with that tender and sympathetic nature which we know upon other grounds to be his.

His *medical interest* has long been noted, and the more so because St. Paul explicitly calls him ' the beloved physician ' (Coloss. iv, 14) ; such a profession, we feel, suited his character, and his character the profession. An almost amusing contrast is afforded by St. Mark's typically downright and vivid language about the woman who ' had suffered much at the hands of many physicians, and had spent all that she had and found no relief, but rather had grown worse '—surely this is not the sort of thing we get from the common source !—whereas St. Luke shows greater consideration for his profession : ' she could not be healed by anyone ' (Luke viii, 43 : Mark v, 26). Early in the Acts all the details about the lame man's trouble and the cure should be remarked (Acts iii, 2–8). We have many examples of his *sympathetic nature*, for example in the story of the widow of Nain (Lc. vii, 11–17) and of St. Paul's last journey to Jerusalem (Acts xx, 36–38 : xxi, 12–14) ; with this we may connect the part which *women* play in his writings, of which the most striking instance is the opening of his gospel (Lc. i–ii ; *cf.* Lc. xxiii, 27–31, 55–56 : Acts ix, 36–43 : xvi, 12–18 : *etc.*). *Universalism* is of the essence of the story of the Acts (i, 8, *etc.*), but finds especial emphasis likewise in the gospel (Luke ii, 32 : iii, 6 : *etc.*). One is tempted to suggest a further likeness between the two works : the gospel may have been written during St. Paul's imprisonment at Caesarea, and the Acts during his imprisonment at Rome. This would also help to explain why St. Luke ends the Acts where he does ; when St. Paul was released from prison he would require once more his faithful follower's active help.

So far the internal evidence has been considered merely to show the common authorship of the gospel and the Acts, though it has furnished some idea of the author's character and bent. The internal evidence of gospel and Acts also

confirms the view that the author is the Luke mentioned by
St. Paul and by all the other external evidence. St. Luke
is named with St. Mark in Philem. 24 and 2 Tim. iv, 11.
More important is the mention of 'Luke, the beloved
physician' in Col. iv, 14, shortly after Mark has been called
'the cousin of Barnabas' (iv. 10). We feel that the descrip-
tion here has some emphasis; St. Luke may well have
ministered to St. Paul as a physician, besides helping him
in the ministry.

We could understand this especial affection all the better
if St. Luke were the author of the 'we-sections,' which
therefore to this extent confirm the attribution to Luke,
besides helping us to understand what must have been the
most momentous period in his life. The term 'we-sections'
is usually applied to those parts of the Acts in which the
writer uses the first person plural, thus indicating his own
presence at the incident related. The first such section is
Acts xvi, 10–17, where the important decision is taken to
cross from Asia to Europe; and we gather that the author
shared St. Paul's counsels in the matter. The scene at
Philippi is vividly described; and from the fact that the
next we-section (xx, 5–xxi, 18) opens at Philipii, we may infer
that the author was left there to develop the church, like
Timothy at Ephesus (1 Tim. i, 3) and Titus in Crete (Tit. i, 5).
So far as the use of the first person plural goes, the third
we-section is xxvii, 1–xxviii, 16; but it is unlikely that the
author lost touch with the Apostle after the second we-
section. There is an isolated and doubtful use of the first
person plural in Acts xi, 28 ('when we were gathered together') found in the Codex Bezae (D), supported, as not
uncommonly happens, by some Old Latin (i.e., pre-Jerome)
evidence, including St. Augustine. This would imply that
the author was at Antioch a good deal earlier than is otherwise indicated, and would confirm the statements of St.
Jerome (De viris illust. VII) and Eusebius (Church History,
Bk. III, chap. 4) that he was a native of that city.

From the we-sections an argument by exclusion can also
be constructed to the Lucan authorship, which, however, fails

to exclude Titus; but Titus has never been put forward as
the author of Acts. A linguistic argument of some weight
can also be put forward in favour of connecting Luke with
Paul, as may be seen in *Horae Synopticae*, pp. 189–190.

St. Luke shows himself throughout a good historian. His
sources are fairly obvious. In the preface to his gospel he
shows himself aware of the advantage of going to eye-witnesses;
and it is natural to suppose that he did so. The we-sections
show that for a large part of the story of St. Paul he could
rely upon his own knowledge; the rest he could easily learn
from the Apostle himself. At the same time he could pick
up the earlier story of the Acts from many in Jerusalem and
elsewhere. The modern craze for documents seems to make
it almost indecent to suggest that for the first two chapters
of his gospel he went to the one person who could tell him
best of all what had happened, and how she had pondered all
these things in her heart; and yet it is hardly doing more
than crediting him with common sense. Of the common
source something has already been said under Mark; but
even those who believe it to be Mark think no worse of Luke
for using it. The ' Logia ' have been briefly discussed under
Matthew, but, once again, even those who would interpret
the word as an early collection of sayings are not inclined
to detract from the authority of such a collection, which
would be common to Matthew and Luke, and answer to the
modern symbol Q. But the evidence is against the existence
of such a collection; on the one hand, the arrangement of the
discourses in Matthew is generally admitted to bear an
artificial character, and, on the other hand, they are scattered
about in Luke in places which often seem likelier to be their
historical setting than their contexts in Matthew.

St. Luke's own contributions are such as to give us confidence in his historical trustworthiness. The first two
chapters of his gospel have already been mentioned; the
simplest and best explanation is that he went to the right
source for them. So has his medical interest, which shows
that he had an eye for accurate detail: a conclusion greatly
strengthened by his account of the final journey to Rome in

Acts, which remains one of the most important texts for ancient ships and sailing. Again, a feature common to gospel and Acts is his frequent mention of rulers : high priests, emperors, Herods, procurators, proconsuls, praetors, politarchs, even a ' first man ' in Malta, this last title justified by a couple of inscriptions. He is lavish of historical and geographical details, and he is not found tripping. The Acts furnish a valuable background to such of the Pauline epistles as fall within the period, and the recorded speeches fit well the circumstances of their delivery. It was indeed an unfortunate remark (from his point of view) of the late Dr. Streeter in *The Four Gospels* (pp. 555–6), that we should assume that the speeches in Acts are ' Thucydidean,' in the sense that ' their real purpose is to afford the historian an opportunity for inculcating ideas which he himself wishes to express.' This is no place to discuss Thucydides, who is thus somewhat hardly used ; it is enough to say that if it be allowed that St. Luke fulfils the ideals expressed by the Greek historian in his famous chapter (Bk. I, chap. 22), no better commendation need be sought for him as a historian.

XV

JOHN

ABOUT the gospel of St. John there are three main views :
the first that it is genuine, the second that St. John had
nothing to do with it, the third that he did not write it but
exercised influence over it. Sanday favoured the 'beloved
disciple,' and Harnack 'John the Presbyter,' but the main
body of the evidence identifies the former with the Apostle,
and even if the latter were distinct from the Apostle, there
is no ancient evidence at all crediting him with the authorship
of the gospel. And it must be remembered that the gospel
is written with great authority, and from the first was accepted without question ; the later it is dated, the more incredible it is that it should have been put on a par with the
other three, unless the Christians were satisfied about its
authorship.

Something has been said in chap. XIII on the evidence to
all four gospels. For John, special emphasis must be laid on
the witness of St. Irenaeus, who takes care to let us know that
he learnt much about St. John from the latter's disciple
Polycarp. He also appeals to other Asiatic presbyters without
naming them ; but it is likely that his predecessor in the see
of Lyons, St. Pothinus, was among them. At the opening
of the fifth book of his *Church History* Eusebius reproduces
the beautiful letter in which the churches of Vienne and
Lyons narrate to the churches of Asia and Phrygia the persecution which befell them in A.D. 177. St. Pothinus was then
more than ninety years old, and died in consequence of the
brutal treatment which he received from the mob. The name
of course is Greek, and he probably came from Asia Minor

like Irenaeus himself; this very letter shows the close
relations between the churches of Asia and Gaul.

It is unnecessary to dwell upon other early evidence. St.
Justin Martyr, early in the second half of the second century,
is full of the doctrine of the *Logos* (' the Word '); and Sanday
in his *Criticism of the Fourth Gospel* (Oxford, 1905) insisted
strongly on the Johannine strain in St. Ignatius of Antioch
(end of first century), quite apart from the single quotation
there found. A recently published papyrus shows the gospel
in book form already in the first half of the second century.[1]
Neither the story of the Apostle's martyrdom at the hands of
the Jews, for which a ninth century chronicler claims Papias
as the source, nor the supposed possibility of there having
been two Johns, really tells against the authorship; but both
of these points are dealt with faithfully in the late Abbot
Chapman's brilliant work *John the Presbyter* (Oxford, 1911).
There is abundant testimony that the Apostle was at Ephesus
in his old age. Abbot Chapman has also shown in the *Journal
of Theological Studies* for July, 1930 (vol. 31, pp. 379–387)
that St. John uses the first person plural for the sake of
solemnity, and always in speaking of his witness (1 John i, 2 :
iv, 14 : III John 12), and even represents Our Lord as doing
the same thing (John iii, 11); nor does he scruple to use
singular and plural verbs together (*cf.* John iii, 11 : III John
9–10). Consequently there is no good reason to doubt that
in John xxi, 24, he is really bearing witness to himself.

Before coming to the strictly internal evidence, it may be
worth noting that textual evidence of itself suffices to throw
back the origin of the fourth gospel into the first century.
The date indicated by Mr. Roberts for his fragment is an
earlier one than used to be assigned to the gospel itself by a
school of critics not so long obsolete. And upon more
general grounds, the two types of text represented by the
Vatican and the Bezan manuscripts (*B* and *D*) respectively
both find such early attestation as once more to compel us
to put their common original into the first century. Both

---

[1] *Cf. An Unpublished Fragment of the Fourth Gospel,* edited by C. H. Roberts,
M.A. Manchester University Press, 1935.

indeed still have their champions, though the superior skill and judgment of the Alexandrian scholars and the superior quality of the readings themselves alike favour the Vatican manuscript.

The gospel was written by a Jew of Palestine contemporary with New Testament times. The time of Our Lord's public ministry was unique, especially in view of the destruction of Jerusalem in 70 A.D., which had an enormous influence on the subsequent development both of Jewry and Christianity : the former lost the Temple, as well as the last vestige of autonomy, while the latter broke loose from Palestine and Judaism more definitely than before. It would not be at all easy after that to reconstruct the New Testament background ; and yet all the evidence goes to show that the writer of the fourth gospel is well at home in it. It is impossible here even to outline the powerful cumulative argument which thus presents itself ; but it has been set forth fully and effectively both by Sanday and Drummond.[1] It is to be regretted that the latter, in a work of over 500 pages, should find no space for the discussion of miracles, but should summarily reject them with an ' unable to believe ' (p. 426) ; but such is still the fashion, not founded directly on any study of the gospel itself.

The author was an Aramaic-speaking Jew, familiar also (as he therefore naturally would be) with the very similar Hebrew language. The style belongs to these languages, the Old Testament quotations show a knowledge of the original Hebrew, Aramaic names are translated, and there are some other features of a less simple character.

The author claims to be an eye-witness (xix, 35 : xx, 30–31 : xxi, 24, already touched upon : cf. 1 John i, 1–3). It is indeed doubtful whether he narrates anything of which he was not an eye-witness, such is the emphasis which he lays upon his own testimony ; and the Beloved Disciple would not easily leave the Master. It is not likely, for example, that he would relate the episode of the Samaritan woman if

[1] Sanday, *Criticism of the Fourth Gospel*, already mentioned ; Drummond, *Character and Authorship of Fourth Gospel*. Williams and Norgate, 1903.

JOHN

he had not stayed by Jesus' side. We may understand John iv, 8, of the main body of the Apostles, not including the actual narrator. In reading his gospel we almost feel his presence from the first, and he asserts it himself at the last.

Only the Twelve were at the Last Supper. Of these, Christ especially loved Peter, James and John, making them the witnesses, for example, of His Transfiguration and Agony. James was early martyred (Acts xii, 2), and the evangelist distinguishes himself from Peter, though implying intimacy (xiii, 24: xx, 2: xxi, 7, 20–21: cf. i, 35–42: Acts iii-iv: viii, 14: Galat. ii, 9).

Before coming to the historical value of the gospel, it may be well to say something about its structure. It appears to have developed gradually from something more like the synoptic gospels. There are parts which obviously came late in the composition. Prefaces are apt to do so, and rightly; St. John's blending into higher unity of the Greek and Jewish 'Word' (or should we not rather say 'Thought'?) was no exception; and it is well-nigh universally recognized that the last chapter of his gospel was a later addition, though not all will admit that he himself was pointing away from himself to Peter and his successors. Again, the departure in John xiv, 31 seems to indicate that cc. xv–xvii are a supplement to the discourse at the Last Supper, to some small extent covering the same ground. On the other hand, the crossing of the Lake of Galilee in John vi, 1, following now upon a scene in Jerusalem, seems best explained by the omission of some account of a Galilaean ministry to make room for these additions; and the account of the multiplication of the loaves and fishes which immediately follows has much of a synoptic style about it. The use of the present tense in John v, 2 (where manuscripts and editors seem to have gone wrong from not realizing that 'Probatic' translates 'Bethzatha') suggests an early date of composition, such as is likewise suggested by the present tense in the epistle to the Hebrews (Hebr. ix, etc.), and confirmed by the obvious references to the epistle in that of St. James. It is important to note that St. John's gospel appears to be the final result of a long growth ; but the argument cannot be developed fully here.

There can be no doubt that the evangelist claims to be trustworthy historically. He asserts his claim emphatically both in the original ending and the final ending of his gospel, and again under the Cross (xix, 35) ; the first epistle attributed to him is so generally acknowledged to be his that its opening words may be added to the passages from the gospel, as a kind of covering letter to which it may well have been issued. So patent is the claim that Dr. Streeter in *The Four Gospels* did not venture to deny that it was made, but contended that the evangelist's purpose was thwarted by ' creative memory ' and ' mystic vision ' (p. 364, *etc.*). This, however, is too desperate an expedient for a work so matter-of-fact in its own narratives and in its handling of the synoptic gospels, with which it clearly supposes the Christians to be already familiar.

In the fourth gospel, far more than in the other three, faith is regarded as based in most cases on miracles, though Our Lord does not regard this as the ideal state of things (iv, 48), and the Baptist did not work any (x, 41). Nathanael received a sign which is not further explained (i, 48–50) : the disciples believe because of the miracle at Cana (ii, 11) : from the beginning the Resurrection is prophesied in veiled terms (ii, 19–22) : Nicodemus declares that no one could work such signs unless God were with him (iii, 2) : the Samaritan woman is told all she had done (iv, 29) : and so on. Another rather striking example of the regard for fact in the gospel is that much is made of the Baptist, which is easily explained if the evangelist was the Baptist's disciple (and perhaps beloved disciple) before being Christ's, but not so easily by ' creative memory ' or ' mystic vision.'

The fact is that the fourth gospel supplements the synoptic gospels in a way that helps to explain the synoptic gospels themselves. It is almost incredible that a would-be Messiah should not have evangelized Judah and Jerusalem, nor yet have attended the great feasts at Jerusalem ; St. John shows that Christ retired to Galilee after failure in the south, but returned for the feasts. The multiplication of the loaves and fishes is the only incident which he repeats from the Galilaean ministry, but obviously with a view to the discourse on the Eucharist. This again is unlike the synoptic discourses, but it explains the bearing of the preceding miracle, and also to a large extent the failure even of the Galilaean ministry. In like manner the raising of Lazarus explains the tremendous enthusiasm of the triumphal entry into Jerusalem.

The task of supplementing is carried out in much detail. The call of the first disciples is given, but not the later constitution of the college of apostles : the promise of the Eucharist, but not the fulfilment : the promise of the Rock-name to Peter, but once again not the fulfilment : only the promise of Peter's headship had been given, and so here St. John gives the fulfilment. The prophecy concerning Bethlehem is mentioned (vii, 42 : *cf.* iv, 44), but the fulfilment was already known. The examination before Annas is given, not the trial before Caiaphas.

A few repetitions there are, but the reason is usually plain, as with that of the multiplication of the loaves and fishes. The supper at Bethany is shown in its historical setting, and throws light upon what the evangelist has to say about the Magdalen and Lazarus and Judas. The denials of Peter are to be atoned by his triple confession. The Passion could hardly be omitted in any case, but much is added ; it becomes clearer, for example, that Pilate was afraid to disregard the accusation that Christ made Himself a king, though he saw that it did not mean revolt. For the Sanhedrin the capital offence was the claim to Divinity, but they did not stop to consider whether it might be true.

St. John also seems at times to be correcting what might be false impressions from the other gospels, as in his remark that Christ was taken first to Annas (xviii, 13), and that He carried His own cross (xix, 17). He is doubtless setting the cleansing of the Temple and the supper at Bethany in their true historical sequence. He shows that the scourging was something more than the usual scourging of a condemned criminal, and gives his own independent version of the denials of Peter, as also of the resurrection. The precise hour of the crucifixion raises some difficulty, if we compare John xix, 14, with Mark xv, 25, but St. John must be presumed to be more precise, as indeed he shows himself elsewhere ; it seems to have been the way to reckon everything up till midday as the third hour. The ancients were far less exact in their reckoning of time than we are, and the genuine oriental has not much changed his ways even now.

Another difficulty arises with regard to the date of the Last Supper, which St. John clearly assigns to the evening before that of the Jewish passover (xviii, 28) ; a double celebration is absolutely excluded even later than this by the rabbinical regulations, which, however, prescribe that the preparations for it should begin the evening beforehand, so that the apostles probably partook the next evening of the passover which had been prepared. Our Lord, on the other hand, certainly meant the Holy Eucharist when He spoke of the passover which He longed to eat with them even before then (Luke xxii, 15). We must remember that the Jewish day began with sunset. There is no difficulty in supposing that Our Lord sent the two apostles to start the passover preparations after sunset, seeing that at an early stage in the proceedings it was already night (John xiii, 30). Even if the apostles were sent before sunset, the date might be intended for the momentous events to follow it. And if all four gospels be carefully examined, the Johannine version seems to fit even the synoptic narratives better than the supposition that Our Lord Himself celebrated a Jewish passover.[1]

Some there are who will insist upon finding contradictions between the fourth gospel and the others ; but this of itself presupposes a historical purpose in St. John, for otherwise his version of events would be irrelevant. Indeed, the meticulous attention which he bestows upon the synoptic narratives have little to remind us of ' creative memory ' or

[1] I have treated the question at some length in an appendix to the first volume of the Westminster Version (New Testament).

JOHN

' mystic vision,' and incidentally rule out any indeliberate
contradiction of them. That he was deliberately contradicting them is neither proved nor probable.

He certainly intends the discourses which he reports to be
taken as historical. Here again Streeter would apply his
' Thucydidean ' standard (*The Four Gospels*, p. 370), of which
enough has already been said. In reality the cases are not
parallel. In John the discourses are the main point, and it
may be said in a general way that the miracles are worked to
justify them ; the two, indeed, combine to form one story
(*cf.* v, 18 with vii, 1, 19 : *etc.*). St. John's preface plainly
gives his own theology ; but it is significant that he never
makes Christ call Himself the Logos ('Word'). Other
passages that appear to be due to St. John himself are
iii, 16–21, 21–36 : xi, 51–52 : xii, 37–41. Doubtless they
all belong to the later strata of the gospel.

In general it must be borne in mind that the gospel implies
for the most part translation (though Our Lord probably
conversed with Pilate in Greek), and that translators usually
keep their own style. It is a summary based on selection
for a special purpose, and for the most part represents Christ
as speaking at Jerusalem to a more or less sophisticated and
hostile audience, or else (at the Last Supper) to His own
apostles, whom He has been training throughout His ministry.
The Eucharistic discourse in a sense proves the rule, since it
is the crisis of rejection in Galilee.

The miracle preceding this discourse is doubtless symbolic,
like some others ; but this confirms, not only the selective
purpose pervading the gospel, but also its historical character,
for there is no sign in the narrative of symbolic heightening.
The miracles themselves, even the raising of Lazarus, are not
more wonderful than those related by the synoptists, though
they are told with greater detail and dramatic effect. The
writer is not incorporating the plain story used in the primitive instruction, but is recording his own experiences with
a simple art learnt from the incomparable tales of the Old
Testament. Some of the miracles, it may be noted, have no
obvious symbolism, though symbolism may be read into

BACK TO THE BIBLE

almost anything by those whose minds are set upon it.
Perhaps the most obviously non-symbolic miracle is that of
the official's son (iv, 46–54). Archbishop Temple, too, in
his *Readings in St. John's Gospel*,[1] records a saying of the late
Canon Scott Holland in regard of the water-pots at Cana
(ii, 1–11): 'You cannot allegorize that water-pot. No one
ever found the Old Law at the bottom of it.'

The gospel has been said to be a work of genius; and who
would deny it? Nevertheless, there is need of some distinction. We do not find in it the all-embracing synthesis
which underlies the epistles of St. Paul; rather we are
presented with a number of great truths faithfully learnt from
the Master, and embodied in the very life of the disciple, but
not explicitly correlated among themselves. The sublime
mentality of St. John is shown rather in the tremendous hold
which he had upon a few doctrines than in their number
or systematic arrangement. In his thought, as in his style,
there is more co-ordination than subordination. In this
he was a true child of the Old Testament; but no prophet
had risen to such divine contemplation. We cannot estimate
him apart from the Incarnate Word, whose intimacy he was
beyond others privileged to share.

We are not surprised, therefore, that the revelation to him
of divine mysteries did not cease with the Ascension. But
it is impossible in this place to discuss the Apocalypse, and
it must be enough to refer to the very full and competent
edition of Père Allo, O.P.,[2] a landmark in the study of the
work. This only may be said, that it thunders from heaven
against the claim to godhead of the Roman emperors. The
menace of totalitarianism goes back to New Testament
times; but it was the less dangerous then because it made no
pretence of Christianity. Nowadays it is a more general
peril.

[1] Vol. I, p. 69. MacMillan, 1941.
[2] *Saint Jean: L'Apocalypse*. Paris, Gabalda, 1921.

XVI

PAUL

Too much stress must not be laid upon the simple men, fishermen and others, upon whom Christ founded His Church. For one thing, the attainments of the apostles should not be unduly depreciated; for another, familiarity with the Old Testament could give them an education and culture which we know to our cost that we are losing. But when according to the divine purpose the time was come for the world to be evangelized, Almighty God chose a man eminently suited for the purpose from outside the apostolic college, as originally constituted, to be His main instrument. St. Paul was a great man upon any standard, in himself and in the effect produced upon the world by his life-work.

We can distinguish in him a threefold culture, fused together in the service of a sublimer mission than any of them could offer him. He was a pharisee born of pharisees, with a faith in the Old Testament which never faltered, faith in the covenants, the Mosaic Law, the Temple liturgy, the promises made to the fathers: faith, therefore, in the Messiah born of them, 'Christ according to the flesh, who is over all, God blessed for ever' (Rom. ix, 5). He saw no inconsistency in his own faith. 'Are we then making void the Law through faith? Heaven forbid! We are establishing the Law' (Rom. iii, 31). Even after he seems to have left nothing to the once Chosen People but divine anger and reprobation, he can still protest, 'God hath not cast off his people whom he foreknew' (Rom. xi, 2):

BACK TO THE BIBLE

There shall come from Sion the deliverer,
  he shall banish impiety from Jacob,
And when I take away their sins,
  this shall be to them my covenant.

(Rom. xi, 26–27.)

But he is a native of Tarsus in Cilicia, politically, com-
mercially, intellectually no mean city, rivalling Athens and
Alexandria as a ' university town.' He evidently owed much
to the Greek, no less than to the Jewish culture, and he had
an utter mastery of the language, straining it almost to
breaking-point in the effort to catch up with the torrent of
his own thought. And that thought was primarily Greek.
No man can keep two languages upon a perfect equality in
his thought ; least of all could Paul maintain such unco-
ordinated and defective languages as Hebrew and Aramaic
(which he yet knew well) upon an equality with the subtle
and sensitive Greek which was ever flashing through his
mind. True, it was a Greek somewhat decadent, if judged
by Attic standards ; but it still remained the most plastic and
perfect expression of human thought that the world has
known.

Finally, Paul was a Roman citizen by birth, though we do
not know how precisely he came to be such : he was one of
the lords of the earth, able to mix on equal terms with the
best provincial society, and not afraid in an emergency to
preserve his life for the work given him by an appeal to his
status. Nor yet did he undervalue the great capital itself,
which rather was the goal of his apostolate, which he had
sought often to reach, though always hindered, till at last
he came as a prisoner (Rom. i, 9–13). There is a virtue sometimes in ' thinking imperially,' and never more so than in
Paul.

His was an emotional character, full of gratitude at the
Philippians' remembrance of him (Philip. iv, 10–20), of anger
at the outrage upon him ordered by the high priest (Acts
xxiii, 3), of ' great sorrow and unceasing grief ' (Rom. ix, 2)
because of the Jews' rejection of their Messiah. His endur-

ance of such suffering both within and without in his zeal for his apostolate was something not alien to his nature, yet the fruit also of an abundance of help accompanying the divine call. Much revelation was imparted to him, and the inspiration of many epistles ; above all, he was a great saint, bringing to ample fruit the graces offered him. If there is one thing that we notice more especially about him, it is his great personal devotion to Christ. No saint can lack this devotion, but in a few it has been so strong as to be a distinguishing characteristic, in a Francis, for example, or an Ignatius ; but beyond all others in Peter and Paul.

St. Paul was the first great Christian missionary, and his especial field was the Aegaean. It is common to speak of his ' missionary journeys ' in a way that is somewhat misleading ; his chief bases were Corinth to the west and Ephesus to the east of the Aegaean. To the north lay Thessalonica and Philippi, and to the south Crete, evangelized last of these. Egypt and Palestine he probably found too Jewish, and even Syria and most of Asia Minor ; there were probably too many Jews and too much judaizing for him even in the Galatian churches. His mission was to the gentiles, not to the Jews. He doubtless went to Spain, for he writes of his intention to do so in Rom. xv, 24, 28 ; the first epistle of Clement, written from Rome itself before the end of the first century, speaks of him as having gone ' to the limits of the west ' (chap. V), and the ' Muratorian fragment,' from about the end of the second century, speaks of his setting out for Spain. It seems likely that he found Spain too Latin for him ; there is no sign that he knew that language.

His epistles fall into six well-defined groups. The earliest extant epistles, the Thessalonian pair, are mainly occupied with Christ's second coming, a subject to which we shall return ; the Apostle found it so disturbing to his Christians that he came to treat of it less and less. The Corinthian epistles yield an instructive picture of the first difficulties of a great church, peculiar in this case from a local tradition at once of ' the wisdom of this world,' emanating from near-by Athens, and a notorious immorality, partly reflected in the epistle to the Romans, written from Corinth. The Galatian and Roman epistles have a controversial character, urging St. Paul's doctrine of a justification based on faith rather than works, as against the excessive emphasis on the latter still to be found in Judaism. His more characteristic and central doctrine is rather to be found in the epistles of the Roman captivity (Ephesians, Colossians, Philippians, Philemon), which dwell upon our corporate identification with Christ, of which immediately. The epistle to the Hebrews is admitted by most to be Pauline at least in the wider sense ; the treatment of the Jewish issue is naturally quite different in an epistle addressed to the Christian Jews themselves. An early date has already been suggested for it in chap. XV. The Pastoral epistles illustrate the Apostle's method in the practical organization of local churches : he sets up a body of priests in each city, subject to visitation from time to time from himself or his delegates. The time was not yet ripe for the establishment of diocesan bishops.

Preaching the gospel meant preaching doctrine ; not only are the epistles full of it themselves, but they presuppose a thorough grounding in it. For the most part St. Paul only touches upon points that need especial explanation or emphasis. The Corinthians enquire about the choice of virginity and celibacy : they are somewhat irreverent in their celebration of the Holy Eucharist : some among them have learnt from Athens to doubt the general resurrection, perhaps even to smile at it : the Apostle is not teaching them for the first time about these matters, but only writing as the occasion requires. And he writes, as he taught, with authority, not usually offering definite proofs, but merely explanations, comparisons, and in general any helpful thoughts that occur to him. Even his doctrine of justification, as has just been said, is drawn from him by the needs of controversy, rather than from any fondness of his own for it. What he wished supremely to teach was Jesus Christ, and Him crucified.

His supreme subject is unity, a synthesis of many aspects. As a practical message for the Christian it meant corporate identity with Christ through faith and baptism. Faith,

PAUL

baptism, justification, incorporation with Christ, were for him one great process, in which he felt no need to introduce subtle distinctions. We have these four elements together, for example, in Galat. iii, 23–29. But to understand the corporate identity with Christ we must needs ponder unity in all its main aspects. Christ is one with the Father; it is because He is both God and man that He can make us also partakers of the Divine Nature. He is one with the Church, His Body, His Bride, even as the Hebrew theocracy was the bride of Jehovah. Man and wife should be one flesh, with one spirit, and with the man for head: the man loves, the wife obeys, thus representing upon earth the mutual relation of Christ and the Church, even as it is the purpose of human fatherhood to show forth, however inadequately, the fatherhood of God (Ephes. iii, 15).

St. Paul does not call the Church the *mystical* body of Christ, nor yet (it seems) do the Fathers of the Church; the epithet is well established now, and fully sanctioned, because a distinction is needed between the Church and the physical Body of Christ, but it has sometimes been used to obscure the fact that the Apostle means a single concrete organism, under a single government. This government belongs to the apostles; and he insists strongly upon his claim to be one of them. He does not mention explicitly St. Peter's primacy, though he may be said to some extent to confirm it: he expounded his doctrine to Peter, James and John, 'for fear I might be running or had run in vain' (Galat. ii, 2, 9), but for these three he presently substitutes Peter alone (Galat. ii, 7). However, his doctrine of the unity of the Church is perfectly clear, quite apart from any mention of St. Peter. Nor must it be thought that St. Paul had any misgivings about the truth of his doctrine—the opening of the epistle (Gal. ii, 1–9) is enough to prove that—but still less could he conceive that his teaching might lawfully be different from that of Peter, James and John.

The unity is one of organization, teaching and ministry. The unity of organization follows from the conception of the Church as Christ's Body, a single organism, as just remarked.

BACK TO THE BIBLE

This conception is most clearly and fully expressed in the epistle to the Ephesians, and gives to that epistle much of its special character. It is found in Ephes. iv, 1–16 : v, 22–23 : the latter passage, dealing with the mutual relation of husband and wife, is in some ways the more explicit, but the emphasis on unity is stronger in the former, being based upon that of the Holy Trinity itself. It is enough to notice here that, as we should put it, there is to be but one soul and one body : the soul is the Holy Ghost, and the body is certainly not understood to consist of disjointed members. In the parallel epistle we may notice especially Coloss. i, 24 : ii, 19. In Rom. xii and 1 Cor. xii, we have the doctrine of the mystical body drawn out at some length, to convey a lesson of mutual charity and harmony.

This one Church is of right universal. In Gal. ii, 7–9 he divides all mankind with Peter, James and John : they are to evangelize the Jews, he the gentiles. In Rom. i, 5, he writes of his mission to all the gentiles : in Rom. x, 8–18, he writes of the universal mission of the Church, and declares it already in large measure fulfilled, as he does likewise in Coloss. i, 6. Omitting other passages, we may draw at once the obvious conclusion that since there is one universal Church, it must be the only Church. What indeed can we say to the suggestion that there can be several, except to ask with the Apostle, ' Is Christ divided ? ' (1 Cor. i, 13).

Such unity could only be maintained by the exercise of authority ; and such authority Paul claimed the right to exercise, in virtue of being an apostle. ' Am I not an apostle ?' (1 Cor. ix, 1). He certainly does not put himself over the other apostles ; as we have seen, he submitted his doctrine to Peter, James and John, and for him the apostolate is the highest order in the Church (cf. 1 Cor. xii, 28 : 11 Cor. xi, 5 : xii, 11 : etc.). Armed with such authority, he threatens to come to the Corinthians with a rod (1 Cor. iv, 21), he bids them excommunicate a culprit (v, 13), he gives some directions about the celebration of the Holy Eucharist, and will give more upon arrival (xi, 34), and is prepared to punish all disobedience (11 Cor. x, 6). Other examples abound.

For him it was the business of the Church, and his own in particular, to teach positive doctrine, and not simply the value of religious experience. The faith which was reckoned justness to Abraham was his faith that Isaac would indeed be born (Rom. iv, 19–21) : the faith demanded of Christians for salvation is chiefly faith in Christ's Godhead and resurrection (Rom. x, 8–18) : the faith whereby they now see in a dark manner, and not yet face to face (1 Cor. xiii, 8–13). This faith he teaches, not relying mainly on proofs, but upon his own apostolic authority. He teaches the Corinthians about virginity (1 Cor. vii), about the Holy Eucharist (cc. x-xi), about the resurrection (chap. XV). It is none the less teaching because he is not always teaching them something new. His epistles, in fact, are steeped in dogma ; it is evident that he looked upon it as his right and duty to teach it. To the Corinthians he writes, ' we overthrow reasonings and every lofty thing that exalteth itself against the knowledge of God, we bring every mind into captivity to the obedience of Christ ' (11 Cor. x, 4–5). ' Unto me,' he writes to the Ephesians, ' hath been given this same grace, to preach to the gentiles the unsearchable riches of Christ ' (Ephes. iii, 8 : the whole context should be read). He identifies his teaching with that of the rest of the apostles (among other places) in Rom. x, 8–18 and 1 Cor. xv, 11 : ' whether therefore I or they, so we preach, and so ye have believed.'

After what has been written there can be no need to insist on the unity of the ministry. As there is but one Lord and one faith, so there is but one baptism (Ephes. iv, 5), making the Christian, as the canon law now says (canon 87), ' a person in Christ's Church, with all the rights and duties of Christians, unless, so far as rights are concerned, an obstacle stand in the way, hindering the bond of ecclesiastical communion, or a censure inflicted by the Church.' In the case of the culprit of 1 Cor. v, there is no question of rebaptism (11 Cor. ii, 7–11). The Holy Eucharist is the seal both of external and internal unity. ' The bread which we break, is it not fellowship in the body of Christ ? We many are one bread, one body, for we all partake of the one bread' (1 Cor. x, 16–17).

In these words there is an indication of that unity of Christians with each other, which follows necessarily from their being members of the one Body and the one Spirit, the Body of Christ, animated by the Holy Ghost. The unity of Christians with Christ Himself is likewise implied, as it is also from their membership of His Body. 'With Christ I am nailed to the Cross; it is no longer I that live, but Christ that liveth in me' (Gal. ii, 19–20). The Christian must be crucified to the world and the world to him (Gal. vi, 14), in order that he may be a new creature. By this strong figure the Apostle endeavours to bring home to his readers the utter renunciation of the old life of sin which is demanded of them, and the immeasurable gulf between that and the divine life now given them. They are fulfilled in Christ, and Christ is fulfilled in them; in this we have a transformation of the soul in its substance and qualities and activities, raising it far beyond its merely natural condition, and making of its body the temple of God.

Most of the letters mentioned so far were written before the synoptic gospels, and by that very fact confirm the historical trustworthiness of those gospels; although the evangelists must have been familiar with a more developed body of doctrine, they do not let it interfere with their faithful report of Our Lord's words and deeds. Pauline influences in the main are conspicuous by their absence, though they do help to explain St. Luke's own standpoint and selections. Even St. John, as has been mentioned towards the end of the chapter dealing with him, has not really been caught up in the Pauline synthesis, nor does he represent Our Lord as expressing Himself in such terms.

The Pastoral Epistles follow later upon the synoptic gospels and upon the other Pauline epistles, though probably not upon the Johannine writings. They are, of course, largely condemned by the 'critics' as un-Pauline—it is so easy to tell what the 'critics' are going to do, but the truth is not always so simple as all that—and yet they have their place in the sweet reasonableness of things, and the other epistles differ so much among themselves that it would not be difficult

PAUL

by such methods to prove almost any one of them un-Pauline. Even the second epistle to Timothy bears a rather different character from the other two Pastoral Epistles, being in the nature of a farewell. But 1 Timothy and the letter to Titus show St. Paul occupied with matters of practical organization, as he was bound to be in the course of time.

We see no trace, here or elsewhere, of the crisis that would inevitably have been produced if the gospels so obviously implied an early end to the world as some would have us believe. In regard of the gospels and Our Lord Himself something has been said at the end of chap. XI. In so far as any crisis can be detected, it is indicated in 11 Thessalonians ; but there St. Paul reproaches his Christians for not knowing better, and for having forgotten his own teaching (11 Thess. ii, 2, 5), and is evidently inclined to ascribe the trouble to false prophets on the spot or forged epistles (11 Thess. ii, 2 : iii, 17).

For our present purpose it will be simplest to find a summary of Pauline eschatology in 1 Cor. xv. Some Athenians had jeered at the idea of the Resurrection (Acts xvii, 32), and clearly something of their spirit had infected the Corinthian Christians. The Apostle insists strongly upon the necessity of belief in the Resurrection, here and (e.g.) in Rom. x, 9 ; there is no need to bring up more passages to prove something so obvious. Nor yet is there need to demonstrate at length that there is to be a general resurrection at the last day ; we read of this in the gospels, and there is a general statement to that effect in 1 Cor. xv, 22 and Acts xxiv, 15, this last the only explicit mention by St. Paul of the analogous resurrection of the wicked. The dead shall rise with a transformed body ; this, of course, must not be so explained as to mean no body at all.

Those who are alive at the last day are not to die ; this is clear from 1 Thess. iv, 17, and also from the right reading in 1 Cor. xv, 51-52 (' we shall not all fall asleep, but we shall all be changed '). So far as words go, St. Paul is evidently numbering himself with those so alive, and is evidently saying that such are not to die. To these two passages we must return. But it is also certain from that rather difficult passage, II Cor. v, 1–10, and especially from verses 4 and 8, that St. Paul would have preferred not to pass through death, but was not at that time certain whether he would do so or not. Not to pass through death, he would have had to live till the last day. He knew that Christ was to judge the living and the dead (II Tim. iv, 1), both those who had died and those who had not, a truth taught also by St. Peter in Acts x, 42 and I Pet. iv, 5, and taken from the New Testament into the creeds.

Some difficulty is occasioned by the reading of the Latin Vulgate in I Cor. xv, 51, which translates, 'We shall all rise again, but we shall not all be changed.' It is reasonably certain that the correct reading is that given in the preceding paragraph; but on account of the official position given by the Council of Trent to the Latin Vulgate, it is generally held by Catholic theologians that it contains no formal error in doctrine of faith or morals. As a matter of fact, the Vulgate itself makes it clear in the other passages already quoted that those who are alive at the last day are not to die, so that it would be contradicting itself if it here asserted the opposite. What probably led to the false reading was the thought of the rising of the great mass of mankind at the final resurrection, as in Rom. viii, 11, and I Cor. vi, 14, and the wish to exclude the damned (of whom the Apostle is not here thinking) from the change to glory here in question. We may therefore be content to interpret the Latin text in this sense; but it has led to some difference of opinion on the doctrine involved, which only the more accurate Pauline scholarship of modern times may be said to have finally resolved.

We now come explicitly to the question whether St. Paul himself expected to be alive on the last day. An affirmative answer is obviously suggested by I Thess. iv, 15, 17, and I Cor. xv, 51–52 (with the correct translation, given earlier). Nevertheless, in regard of both passages we have reason to pause; the Apostle, as has already been noted, was not pleased with the Thessalonians' over-eager expectation of the end (cf. II Thess. ii, 1–6), and in I Cor. vi, 14, he actually numbers

himself this time among those who will be dead. Clearly he
had no certain knowledge on the point, as is shown beyond
doubt in II Cor. v, 1–10, already touched upon.

There are other passages also to be mentioned, but before
coming to them it may be clearer to consider at once how he
could use the first person plural in the two passages just
mentioned. In the first place, he seems to be answering the
Thessalonians according to the terms of their question or
difficulty. Some, probably most, of the Thessalonians expected the end to come soon, and some were giving up their
regular work in consequence (cf. II Thess. iii, 10–15); but
meanwhile they were anxious about their dead, fearing apparently that they would have no part in the triumph of the
Lord's coming. St. Paul assures them that the dead are
to rise with glorified bodies even before the living have their
own bodies transformed (I Thess, iv, 15–17). The distinction is thus between ' us the living ' and the dead, and it is
with the fate of the latter that the Apostle is mainly concerned ;
he does not stop to tell the Thessalonian Christians that they
themselves may be in the other category, among the dead.
Something of the same sort is doubtless true of the Corinthians, especially as we know that they had been sending
enquiries to Paul (I Cor. vii, 1); but it has already been
mentioned that in this epistle he numbers himself also among
those who will be dead at the last day (vi, 14), showing that
he did not wish to lay down anything for certain on the point.

This last passage is further borne out by II Cor. iv, 14,
and also by Rom. viii, 11. We must also take into account
Rom. xi, 25–32, a plain prophecy of the mass-conversion of
the Jews before the last day. So long as such a mass con-
version was not taking place, we know from Paul's own words
that he could not have been expecting the end ; nor for the
same reason can we expect it now, in spite of the various
Antichrists pointed out from time to time.

' As for me, already I am poured out in sacrifice, and the
time of my departure is at hand ' (II Tim. iv, 6). When we
take our leave of him in the New Testament, all doubt has
passed away, and he faces impending martyrdom, looking

forward to that ' crown of justness which the Lord, the just judge, shall award to me on that day, and not only to me, but to all who have loved his appearing.' The final triumph of Christ the Lord is to be regarded, not only with awe, but likewise with love and desire. It is upon this note that the New Testament ends: ' Amen! Come, Lord Jesus! ' (Apoc. xxii, 20).